Lucian of Samosata

Dialogues of Lucian

The Sale of Lives

Lucian of Samosata

Dialogues of Lucian
The Sale of Lives

ISBN/EAN: 9783741140426

Manufactured in Europe, USA, Canada, Australia, Japa

Cover: Foto ©Andreas Hilbeck / pixelio.de

Manufactured and distributed by brebook publishing software (www.brebook.com)

Lucian of Samosata

Dialogues of Lucian

Vol. II

Dialogues of Lucian

From the Greek

London, Printed in the Year 1779
for the Company at Holborn

ADVERTISEMENT.

HAVING no better excuse to make for the appearance of this Second Volume than the favourable opinion of the Publisher; I am, therefore, the Reader may conclude, not very unwilling to admit what has been advanced by a great Author, that BOOKSELLERS ARE NOT THE WORST JUDGES OF BOOKS.

J. C,

i

THE
SALE
OF
LIVES.

A

THE
SALE OF LIVES.

JUPITER.

SET the benches, Mercury, and get ready the room against people come. And bring forward the Lives, and place them in due order. And—do you hear?—let them put on their [*a*] best looks, that we may make the

[*a*] When slaves were carried to market, they were always dressed to the utmost advantage; that is, as the English proverb well expresses it, they were made as fine as a horse, and for the same reason. There is another way of setting off things to advantage, which auctioneers are not unacquainted with. This is what Phædria in Terence means by " munus " nostrum ornato verbis quod poteris." Eunuch. II.

most of them. Come, make proclamation, call together the company, and give a general invitation to all such as wish to receive the favours of fortune.—We are going, gentlemen, to dispose of a choice collection of philosophers of all sorts and sizes; and, if any one of you find it inconvenient to pay ready money for what he buys, he shall be indulged with a year's credit, on giving proper security.

MERCURY.

Here is already a good appearance of company: what need of further delay?

JUPITER.

Very well; let us begin then.

MERCURY.

Which of them will you have first?

JUPITER.

The Ionian, that well-looking gentleman with the fine hair.

MERCURY.

Come down, Mr. Pythagoras, and shew yourself.

JUPITER.

Proceed, Mercury.

MERCURY.

This, gentlemen, is a [b] capital lot; every thing that is respectable and excellent! Who buys? Who wishes to be more than man? Who wants to be acquainted with the [c] harmony of the universe? or to live after he is dead?

BUYER.

His appearance is far from being despicable. In what does his knowledge principally consist?

[b] Joannes Bourdelotius, remarking on this passage, quotes many authorities to prove, that it has always been usual for the seller to praise his goods. Does he not also at the same time prove his near kindred to an author mentioned by Cicero, who wrote a book to convince the world, that none of the great generals of antiquity could have won so many battles without men? Cicero de Officiis.

[c] According to Pythagoras, the universe consists in harmony, all things joining to make up a concert. The musick of the spheres, as they rolled over his head, was (to him) very audible and distinct. See Diogenes Laertius, Cicero de Natura Deorum, Jamblichus, &c.

MERCURY.

He underſtands arithmetick, aſtronomy, geometry, muſick, juggling, ſtory-telling: he deals much in the marvellous; and, in ſhort, is a cunning man.

BUYER.

May one put a queſtion to him?

MERCURY.

By all means. In the name of fortune, why not?

BUYER.

What countryman are you, Sir?

PYTHAGORAS.

A Samian.

BUYER.

Where had you your education?

PYTHAGORAS.

Amongſt the wiſe men of Ægypt.

BUYER.

Well, if I ſhould purchaſe you, what will you teach me?

PYTHA-

PYTHAGORAS.

I shall teach you nothing; I shall only put you in [*d*] mind.

BUYER.

Put me in mind! I do not understand you. What do you mean? How will you do it?

PYTHAGORAS.

I shall begin by purging your soul, and washing it clean from its filth.

BUYER.

But supposing me to be already purged, what is your method of putting in mind?

PYTHAGORAS.

I make a beginning with peace and quietness, prohibiting the utterance of a single syllable for five whole years together.

BUYER.

You might have been a very fit preceptor for the son of Cyrus. But I, who have the use of

---

[*d*] To persons who have lived as many lives as Pythagoras, *teaching*, it seems, is only *putting them in mind* of what they already know.

my tongue, wifh to preferve it: I do not want your inftructions to become a ftatue.—But what is to be done next, after fo long a filence, after being mute for five whole years?

PYTHAGORAS.

You are then to apply yourfelf to mufick and geometry.

BUYER.

A very natural way of proceeding! firft a fiddler, and then a philofopher!

PYTHAGORAS.

Next comes arithmetick.

BUYER.

I underftand arithmetick already.

PYTHAGORAS.

Do you? How do you reckon?

BUYER.

One, two, three, four.

PYTHAGORAS.

Observe what I say, Sir. Your one, two, three, four, are ten. It is a [e] perfect triangle, which I swear by.

BUYER.

By the greatest of all oaths, the sacred number Four, I swear I never heard such divine conversation before!

PYTHAGORAS.

Next, Sir, you shall be made acquainted with what relates to earth, air, water, fire; whither they tend, what is their form, and whence they derive their motion.

BUYER.

Form! Has fire, or air, or water, any form?

---

[e] The number Ten, placed in the following manner, make an equilateral Triangle:

Ναι μα τοι αμιλιξς ψυχα παραδοιλα τιλρακλιν,
Παραν αιιναου φυσιος.   Pythag. Golden Verses.

PYTHAGORAS.

Ay, certainly, and figure too. How elfe could they move? But this is all nothing. You fhall be made to underftand that the Divinity itfelf is nothing more than Number and Harmony.

BUYER.

Truly, you furprize me.

PYTHAGORAS.

Befides all this, you fhall be taught to know that you yourfelf, who feem to be only yourfelf, are not yourfelf as you appear to be.

BUYER.

How?—What? not myfelf! Am not I, who now converfe with you, myfelf? Or am I somebody elfe?

PYTHAGORAS.

Why, at prefent, to be fure, you may be faid to be yourfelf. But there was a time when you were not. You appeared in quite a different body, and went by another name; as you will do again in due time.

BUYER.

BUYER.

You mean, I suppose, that I am to last for ever, only going through a succession of various forms. But I will not urge you farther on this head. With regard to your manner of living——

PYTHAGORAS.

I do not eat animal food; but have no objection to any thing else, except beans.

BUYER.

Why dislike beans?

PYTHAGORAS.

It is not dislike; they are sacred and awful, their nature is [*f*] mysterious. In the first place, the whole is generative. If you shell a bean, whilst it remains unripe, you will perceive in it a near resemblance to certain parts of a man's body. And, if you boil it, after being exposed to the air a certain number of moonlight nights, it will become blood. More than that, the Athe-

---

[*f*] See Diogenes Laertius, p. 222. also Jamblichus, p. 91, &c. and Porphyry, p. 43. Editio Amstelodensis.

nian law directs the choice of their magistrates to be made by beans.

BUYER.

Most nobly and divinely spoken! But, strip; I want to see you naked. As I am here, a golden thigh! No mortal surely! he is some [g] god! Let me have him. What is his price?

MERCURY.

Ten [b] Minæ.

BUYER.

I will take him at that price.

JUPITER.

Write down the name and country of the buyer.

MERCURY.

He seems to me to be an Italian: I suppose, he comes from Croton, or Tarentum, or thereabouts. But what am I talking of? Pythagoras does not fall to one man's lot; for there

---

[g] Εσσεαι αθανατος Θεος αμβροδος, και Σιτιος.
                                Pythag. Golden Ver.
[b] Thirty-two pounds, five shillings and ten-pence.

are about three hundred who no doubt are to have every one a share of him.

JUPITER.

Let them take him. Bring another.

MERCURY.

Will you have that dirty fellow from Pontus [i]?

JUPITER.

Yes.

MERCURY.

Hark you, Sir, you with the wallet, with your shoulder peeping through your cloak; come, and shew yourself round to the company. Here's your manhood, and spirit, and virtue, and liberty! Who buys?

BUYER.

Liberty! Do you undertake to sell Liberty, Mr. Auctioneer? Would you put up a free man?

MERCURY.

I do.

[i] Diogenes, the Cynick, born at Sinope, a city of Pontus.

BUYER.

BUYER.

And are you not afraid of being called to account for kidnapping? Have you not before your eyes the fear of the court of Areopagus?

MERCURY.

He does not allow, Sir, that any thing can affect his liberty; so he does not regard being sold. Wherever he is, or whatever he is, he insists upon it he is always free.

BUYER.

What could one do with such a slaven? unless, perhaps, he might serve to delve, or carry water?

MERCURY.

Yes; and if you should have occasion for him as a door-keeper, you will find him as faithful to the full as his [k] namesake.

BUYER.

What countryman is he, and what does he profess?

MERCURY.

Your best way will be to ask himself.

[k] The dog.

BUYER.

BUYER.

So I might, perhaps, if I were not afraid of him. He is very furly, and looks as if he would bark at leaft, if not bite. Only mind how he grafps his cudgel, and knits his brows. He means no good, depend upon it, for he is brimfull of ire.

MERCURY.

O never fear his looks: he is tame enough.

BUYER.

Pr'ythee, honeft friend, what countryman?

DIOGENES.

An Everywhereian.

BUYER.

What do you fay?

DIOGENES.

I fay, I am a citizen of the world.

BUYER.

And a follower of whom?

DIOGENES.

Of Hercules.

BUYER.

BUYER.

I see you are provided with a club like Hercules; but where is your lion's skin?

DIOGENES.

O Sir, my old cloak does very well for that. I make war on pleasure, as he did, but with this difference, that I am a volunteer in the work of reformation, and do not go about purging the world by compulsion [*l*].

BUYER.

You are engaged in a most laudable enterprise. But by what art or science would you be distinguished?—what would you choose to be called?

DIOGENES.

The deliverer of mankind; the physician of the passions. In short, my profession is, truth and plain dealing.

[*l*] Hercules, as it is well known, was set to work by Eurytheus, king of Mycenæ; who, to please Juno, enjoined him the most hazardous undertakings, in hopes of getting him knocked on the head.

BUYER.

BUYER.

Suppose then, Mr. Plain-dealer, I should make a purchase of you, what method would you take with me?

DIOGENES.

First of all, I would strip you. Not a remnant of your luxury would I leave you. I would wrap an old cloak about your shoulders, and confine you to poverty. I would oblige you to labour and toil; to make your bed of the bare ground; to drink pure water, and to fill your belly with whatever falls in your way. As for money, if you should chance to have any, I would advise you to toss it into the sea. Totally regardless of wife and children, and country, you are to look upon human life as a jest [*m*]. Having quitted your father's house, you will be commodiously lodged in a [*n*] tomb, an old

---

[*m*] παντα ληρος, all things a jest.
"Life is a jest, and all things shew it."
Gay's Monument.

[*n*] That tombs were not always appropriated to the dead alone, but occasionally the habitation of poor and disorderly

tower, or a tub. Your wallet shall be filled with lupines, and books [o] full of writing. With all these blessings you may very well declare yourself happier than any king in the universe. A whip, or a rack, may chance to fall to your share; but trifles like these, which give no trouble, will not be worth your attention.

BUYER.

No! what, do you think I am to have no feeling? Or, do you think I am cased like a crab, or a tortoise?

DIOGENES.

You must proudly repeat the verse of Euripides, only altering it a little.

BUYER.

What verse?

persons, appears from such authority as is not to be quoted here. In our own times bulks, glasshouses, and the mint, have been the dormitories of men of wit. See Dr. Johnson's life of Richard Savage. It was in the vault of her deceased husband, that the inconsolable dame of Ephesus indulged her grief.   Petronius Arbiter.

[o] οπισθογραφοι, books written on the outside as well as the inside, not to make any waste of paper, as rich men are wont to do.

Scriptus et in tergo, necdum finitus Orestes.
                                    Juvenal. Sat. I. v. 6.

SALE OF LIVES. 19

DIOGENES.

[b] My heart is full, but then my tongue's at
ease. Your greatest accomplishments, and which
are indeed indispensable, will be, to appear ex-
cessively impudent and audacious, to abuse
every body in turn; to snarl at all mankind,
gentle and simple, from the king to the cobler. Sparing none, you will be gazed at by
all, and admired as most intrepid. Your voice
must be barbarous, your dictates harsh, growl-
ing, and surly as the salutation of a mastiff.
You must take care to screw up your countenance, and let your gait be in strict conformity
with your looks. In one word, you are to be
as much a savage as a bear, and are to take care
that you be always in character. To all mo-
desty, gentleness, and moderation, you are to
bid a final adieu. Leave no where a spot in
your face that can be disgraced with a blush.
Frequent the most public places. Be there
always alone. Condescend not to have the least
communication or society with friend or stranger. That would be to discover your real cha-

[b] Ἡ γλῶσσ' ὀμώμοχ', Ἡ δὲ φρὴν ἀνώμοτος.

Eurip. Hip. 6r.

B 2   racter,

racter, and of course to destroy all your [*q*] consequence. You are to do actions with the utmost confidence before the eyes of all the world, which another man even in private would blush to think of. In your amorous intercourse there is to be as little propriety as possible. Last of all, when you grow tired of yourself, you may then think good to treat yourself with a raw polypus, or a cuttle fish. Such is the happiness I would set before you.

MERCURY.

How you run on! I wonder you are not ashamed of talking in this manner!

DIOGENES.

Hold, Sir. I can say this for my speculations, that they are easily reduced to practice, and suited to every capacity. I point out a short cut to glory, without obliging you to have recourse to education, or waste your time with the

[*q*] Alluding to certain mysteries of state, which are of no little use in the art of government.
† Such was the end of Diogenes. See Diogenes Laertius, 156.

tiresome

tiresome learning of trifling books. Any ordinary ignorant fellow of a common handicraft trade, a cobler, a seller of saltfish, a smith, or money-lender, may learn of me to become illustrious; he has only to acquire a sufficient stock of impudence, insolence, and ill language, to set up with.

BUYER.

Although I do not find myself in need of any such instructions; yet, as you may possibly some time or other be made good for something, may serve to plant cabbage, or ply an oar, I do not much care if I become a purchaser. But I cannot think of giving above two oboli at most.

MERCURY.

I wish you joy of him! take him at your own price. He has kept up such a continual disturbance, has made such a clamour, such a roaring, is so very abusive, and so ill-mannered to every body, that, I do assure you, we shall not be at all sorry to be fairly rid of him.

JUPITER.

Bring another, that [r] Cyrenæan, with the purple and garland.

[r] Aristippus.

MERCURY.

Now, good people, I beg of you all to attend. This is a lot worth your money; a lot for the rich. This is a sweet, a delicious life. Who loves what is elegant? Who buys a fine gentleman?

BUYER.

Come, Sir, be pleased to inform us what you know. I mean to buy you, if I find you likely to be useful.

MECURY.

I must beg of you, Sir, not to trouble yourself with asking him questions: you see the gentleman has been drinking, and is not altogether capable at present of giving you an intelligible answer.

BUYER.

Who in his senses would defire to buy such a bargain; an abandoned libertine; a slave to pleasure? The man is all over essence and perfume! How he totters! He hardly keeps himself on his feet, and is no longer in a capacity of proceeding straight forward. Tell us, Mercury,

cury, what are his properties, and where lies his skill?

MERCURY.

To give you his character in a few words: he is a boon companion, a jolly fellow, can sing, and dance, and drink, and roar. He would be a good second to a musick-girl; a very fit associate for some thoughtless man of pleasure. I must not omit to mention, that he is well skilled in the art of cookery; knows perfectly well what is good, and how to prepare it. In short, he is an accomplished minister of pleasure. The gentleman was bred at Athens, and afterwards gained great reputation in the service of the Sicilian tyrants. This is a summary of his doctrine: Despise every thing, make the most of every thing, seek pleasure in every thing.

BUYER.

You must look about for a monied man to buy him: he is not a purchase for me.

MERCURY.

I am afraid, Jupiter, this is a bargain likely to lie on our hands.

JUPITER.

Set him by, and bring another. Stay, let us have these two in one lot, the [s] laughing Abderite, and the [t] weeping Ephesian: I will have them go together.

MERCURY.

Come down then, you two. Here, gentlemen, you have a pair of lives not to be paralleled; the wisest in all the world.

BUYER.

O Jupiter, what a contrast! One of them laughs without ceasing, while the other weeps, and seems as full of woe as if he had lost his best friend. You, Sir, what makes you titter so?

---

[s] Democritus, a native of Abdera.
[t] Heraclitus, a native of Ephesus.

DEMOCRITUS.

What makes me titter so, say you? I laugh, Sir, because I cannot forbear; you and your actions are both so ridiculous.

BUYER.

What, all of us? Do you pretend to laugh at all mankind? And is the amount of all we do just nothing at all?

DEMOCRITUS.

The matter is even so. There is nothing solid or substantial in human life: all is an empty jumble, a blind impulse of atoms.

BUYER.

It may be so in your brain, I believe. Leave off your sneering, for shame!—But it will be better to speak to your companion. Pray, my good friend, why do you weep so?

HERACLITUS.

I weep, Sir, because whatever relates to man is full of misery and sorrow; I pity and bewail a fatality from which nothing is exempt. Of the present I can say nothing good; and the future,

future, I forefee, will be wretched indeed. I fpeak of the conflagration, and the cataftrophe of the univerfe. I may well weep when I fee nothing permanent, nothing durable; nothing to be found confiftent with itfelf; pain and pleafure are the fame thing; knowledge is ignorance; great is little; upwards and downwards continually changing; turning and winding dances the whirligigg of life.

BUYER.

Pray what is life?

HERACLITUS.

A child at play; a reftlefs gamefter toffing the dice.

BUYER.

And what are men?

HERACLITUS.

Mortal Gods.

BUYER.

And what are Gods?

HE.

HERACLITUS.

Immortal men.

BUYER.

You speak paradoxes, and are so ænigmatical, that an oracle cannot be more obscure. Really, Mr. Apollo, there is no understanding you.

HERACLITUS.

And what do I care whether you do or no? I do not trouble my head with any of your concerns.

BUYER.

If that is the case, I think no man in his senses will wish to buy you.

HERACLITUS.

What do I care for that? I only wish all all mankind, without distinction, young and old, buyers or not buyers, to weep and wail together.

BUYER.

BUYER.

If this be not madness, it is something very like it. I will have nothing to do with either of them.

MERCURY.

So, they also remain unsold!

JUPITER.

Put up another.

MERCURY.

What do you say to the prating [u] Athenian?

JUPITER.

Let us have him.

MERCURY.

Come hither, Sir. This is a life good and wise. Who buys a piece of sanctity?

BUYER.

Pray what is it you profess? What are you best acquainted with?

[u] Socrates.

SOCRATES.

I am thoroughly skilled in whatever [*] relates to love.

BUYER.

O your servant! I have done. I have a fine boy, and wanted a tutor for him.

SOCRATES.

And where could you hope to meet with a person more fit for your purpose? I am an admirer of intellectual, not corporeal beauty. You will hear no complaints of me respecting my attachment to the latter, even from those who live with me in the most unreserved familiarity.

BUYER.

A very likely story! a lover of youth and beauty attentive only to the soul! and in such circumstances too as you have instructed me to suppose!

[*] See Plato, Cornelius Nepos, &c. A reader, acquainted with the original, cannot fail to observe, that, throughout the whole of this translation, any mention of a certain odious vice has been as much as possible avoided.

SOCRATES.

I swear by the [y] Dog and the Plane tree, that it is even so as I say.

BUYER.

And I swear by Hercules, that you appeal to very ridiculous divinities

SOCRATES.

Take care what you say. I hope you allow the Dog to be a divinity. And what do you think of Anubis? Consider what a figure he makes in Ægypt. Sirius is reverenced in Heaven above, and Cerberus in Hell below.

BUYER.

I beg pardon: I had forgot myself. But what is your way of life?

---

[y] Socrates, it seems, did not hold these deities less respectable than many others.

SOCRATES.

[z] I inhabit a city of my own founding; I have introduced a new form of government, and I make my own laws.

BUYER.

I should be glad to have a sample of your legislation.

SOCRATES.

I will mention to you one of the most important of my institutions concerning women. I ordain, that no woman shall be deemed the peculiar property of any one man, but ready and willing to oblige every one who likes her with every favour in her power to bestow.

BUYER.

What, are the laws against adultery then to be considered as null and void?

---

[z] This, and what follows, alludes to the Republick, &c. of Plato. Plato is generally supposed to have expressed the sentiments of his master Socrates, who published nothing himself. He was too wife to write books.

SOCRATES.

Ay, certainly, all that trifling is at an end.

BUYER.

What is your pleasure with respect to youth of the other sex?

SOCRATES.

My pleasure is, that the publick bestow them as a recompence to such as shall deserve them by distinguished actions.

BUYER.

A very bountiful legislator! And what do you say is the principal wisdom?

SOCRATES.

Ideas and models of existence. Beyond the boundaries of the universe are certain invisible images of all that you see, of the earth, and of every thing upon it, of the sea, and of the sky.

BUYER.

Where are they, do you say?

SOCRATES.

No where. If they were any where, they would not be at all.

BUYER.

I cannot perceive any of them.

SOCRATES.

I do not wonder at that: the eye of your underſtanding is blind. But I contemplate the images of all things. I do not perceive you as you appear. I ſee myſelf a perſon different from myſelf. To me all things appear double.

BUYER.

You are ſo very wiſe, and can ſee ſo well, that I muſt have you.—Hark you, Mercury, what do you aſk for him?

MERCURY.

Two [z] talents.

BUYER.

He is mine; you ſhall have the money for him.

[z] 397 *l.* 10 *r.*

MERCURY.

Pray, what is your name?

BUYER.

I am [a] Dion, of Syracuse.

MERCURY.

Take him, with twenty [b] good lucks.— I shall next put up the Epicuræan. Who will buy him? He is a disciple of the [c] Laugher and the Toper, two lots just sold. But he ventures to carry matters farther than his masters, being somewhat more profane. As to what re-

---

[a] The reader is to understand what is here said of Socrates as applicable to Plato, for whom, as we are informed by Cornelius Nepos, Dion had a most extravagant regard; and, by the favour of Dionysius, enjoyed his company and conversation. Dionysius, however, not being himself equally charmed with his new acquaintance, ordered him to be sold for a slave. Accordingly, as Diodorus Siculus informs us, he was sold in the market for twenty minæ, equal to 64l. 11s. 8d. Had he been sold as a philosopher, perhaps he would not have fetched so much.

[b] Αγι λαβων αγαθη τυχη is the original. The translation was taken from the mouth of a country auctioneer.

[c] Democritus and Aristippus. From the former he learnt the doctrine of atoms, from the latter his theory of pleasure.

mains of his character; he is a good-humoured fellow, and a dear lover of good living.

BUYER.

What is the price of him?

MERCURY.

[*d*] Two minæ.

BUYER.

Here is your money. Pray what kind of food does he prefer?

MERCURY.

He loves any thing sweet; any thing that tastes of honey; but his favourite repast is figs.

BUYER.

If that be all, I can easily supply him. I will buy him whole frails of figs from Caria.

JUPITER.

Call another. Let us have that smooth-pated, sour-looking [*e*] stoick.

[*d*] Six pounds, nine shillings, and two pence.
[*e*] Chrysippus.

MERCURY.

You are in the right, Jupiter; for there seems to be a great number of chapmen for him. I am going, gentlemen, to sell you Virtue itself. This is indeed a life of lives. Who wants to have all knowledge centered in himself alone?

BUYER.

What do you mean?

MERCURY.

I mean, Sir, that this man is the only [ƒ] wise man; the only handsome man; the only just man; the only valiant man; the only king; the only orator; the only rich man; the only legislator; the only every thing——

BUYER.

The only cook; the only cobler; the only carpenter, and so forth!

MERCURY.

Yes.

[ƒ] Ad summum sapiens uno minor est Jove, dives,
Liber, honoratus, pulcher, rex denique regum;
Præcipue sanus—nisi cum pituita molesta est.

Hor. Epist. L

BUYER.

Come down, dread Sir, and tell me, as I mean to bid money for you, what you think of yourself. In the first place, pray would not you take it very heinously to be sold for a slave?

CHRYSIPPUS.

No, not at all. Whatever does not depend on ourselves is to be considered as [g] indifferent.

BUYER.

I do not understand you.

CHRYSIPPUS.

No! What, do not you know that some things are [h] preferred; others rejected?

BUYER.

Not I; you grow more and more obscure.

CHRYSIPPUS.

Possibly. You have not been accustomed to our terms, and are deficient in the faculty of

[g] See Epictetus, near the beginning.
[h] See Cicero de Finibus, III. 4.

com-

[*i*] comprehenſion. But the adept, profoundly read in dialecticks, not only knows all this, but is alſo well acquainted with accident and præter-accident, and can tell how and in what they differ.

BUYER.

In the name of philoſophy, I beſeech you, do not grudge ſome ſmall explication of your ac-

[*i*] It is not always eaſy to preſerve the alluſions to the ſtoical cant, which is here meant to be ridiculed. Thoſe minute inquiſitors,

"Who would keep us in the pale of words till death,"

might in this dialogue find ſome little employment, in nicely diſtinguiſhing words with and without an alluſion.

It was objected to the former volume of this tranſlation, by a very learned and valuable man, that the notes contained no verbal criticiſm. If the obſervation had come from any other than a friend, it might have been replied, that verbal criticiſm, uſeful as no doubt it often is, is not of the moſt difficult attainment; nor does it ſeem to be in its proper place, when employed upon Lucian. Rather let ſome graver author find food for philological maſtication. The wry words of Lucian are not thus to be ſet ſtraight.

To make a ſhew of verbal criticiſm, nothing more would be neceſſary than to prune the luxuriant opuſcula of Hemſterhuſius, Jenſius, Grævius, &c. &c. " quæ legat cui bonas horas perdere libet." Peace to all ſuch!

cident

cident and præteraccident. You cannot think how I am struck with the order and flow of your words.

CHRYSIPPUS.

O, I will teach you the difference with all my heart. When a lame man unawares gets a wound by hitting his lame foot against a stone, the lameness is an accident, but the wound is a præteraccident.

BUYER.

Most wonderful acuteness! And in what else does your wisdom chiefly consist?

CHRYSIPPUS.

I am conversant in all the [k] mazes of speech, and bewilder those who converse with me. I shut up their mouths; I silence; I muzzle them. The wonderful faculty, by which I effect all this, is called Syllogism, the famous Syllogism.

[k] Chrysippus had several names for his different species of argumentation; such as, Sorites, Mentiens, Crocodeilites, Cornuta, Electra, Ignava, Achilles, Metens, Dominans, Nemo, and others, which even the subtle brain of Aristotle was unable scientifically to attain.

BUYER.

By Hercules, Sir, you grow moſt potent! your argumentation is invincible.

CHRYSIPPUS.

Hark you! Have you a child?

BUYER.

What of that?

CHRYSIPPUS.

If he ſhould happen to be walking by the ſide of the river, and a [/] crocodile ſhould chance to lay hold of him, on condition of letting him go again provided you give a true anſwer, when he aſks you what he is reſolved on; what do you think you ſhould ſay?

[/] The ſophiſm called a Crocodile took its riſe, they ſay, from the following ſtory: A gipſey walking on the banks of the Nile had the misfortune to have her little boy laid hold of by a crocodile. She begged and prayed him to let him go, till at laſt the crocodile promiſed, that, if ſhe gave him a true anſwer to a queſtion, ſhe ſhould have her boy again. The queſtion he aſked her was, Will I reſtore your ſon to you or no? The reader ſees what a dilemma the poor woman was reduced to, ſince the truth of her anſwer depended altogether on the will of the crocodile.

BUYER.

BUYER.

I should be at my wit's end: I do not know what I could say to get my child again. Do you, for Heaven's sake, make a proper reply, and save him. Whilst I am beating my brains for an answer, the poor child may be devoured.

CHRYSIPPUS.

You have no manner of occasion to be alarmed. But, Sir, this is nothing to what I shall teach you.

BUYER.

What more have you to instruct me in?

CHRYSIPPUS.

The [m] Reaper, and the [m] Ruler; and, what is still more, [m] Electra, and the [m] Hidden.

BUYER.

What do you mean? Who is the Hidden, and who is Electra?

[m] These cant terms for so many kinds of argumentation have been already remarked. We are informed by Diogenes Laertius, that he gave one pound, twelve shillings, and three-pence half-penny, to learn Θιριζων, the Reaper.

CHRY-

CHRYSIPPUS.

Electra, the [*n*] daughter of Agamemnon, was at the same instant acquainted with and ignorant of the very same thing. She knew very well that Orestes was her brother, but knew not that he who stood by her was Orestes. But you shall hear the other; the Hidden. The Hidden is very wonderful. Answer me this question: Do you know your own father?

BUYER.

To be sure I do.

CHRYSIPPUS.

But, if I should produce you a man in a mask, and ask you if you know him, what would you say?

BUYER.

What would I say? I would say, No.

CHRYSIPPUS.

But, the man masked being your father, if you knew not him, it is very plain that you do not know your own father.

[*n*] See the Electra of Sophocles. Act. IV. Scene I.

BUYER.

BUYER.

I deny it; becaufe, only unmafk him, and I
fhall then know him immediately. But, tell
me, what is the end propofed by this your wif-
dom? and what is to be done when you attain
the fummit of virtue?

CHRYSIPPUS.

I fhall attach myfelf to fuch things as nature has made my principal concern. I mean,
I fhall ftudy riches, and health, and other advantages. But firft of all, it is neceffary to
take great pains; to labour and toil; to pore
over books of which the characters are fo fmall
as to be fcarcely legible. It is equally neceffary
to bundle up the conjectures of fcholiafts, and
to be crammed with folœcifm and abfurdity.
But after all, there is no being completely a
wife man without three dofes of Hellebore
fwallowed in due order.

BUYER.

All very fine and very fenfible! But of Gniphon the ufurer, the dirty Gniphon, ([o]) this

---

[o] Chryfippus had juft mentioned riches as one of the moft
laudable purfuits of a wife man's life.

is not digressing from the subject, I believe) of him what shall we say? Shall we speak of him as of one who has been regularly drenched with hellebore, and perfect in virtue?

CHRYSIPPUS.

Certainly. Usury is a practice becoming the wise man alone. To collect arguments and to collect interest are nearly akin, and both much in his way. Neither should his industry be satisfied with simple interest. Interest on interest, compound interest is the thing for him. You cannot but know, that of interest there is the first and the second, and that the second is the offspring of the first. Now be pleased to attend to the instruction contained in a Syllogism. If you admit the first proposition, you must the second. If the wise man receives the first interest, he will the second: But he receives the first; ergo he will the second.

BUYER.

Then with regard to the money which you take for instructing youth—but it is as plain as plain can be, that the wise man has no other motive in receiving money than only as it serves to promote virtue.

CHRY-

CHRYSIPPUS.

Now I see you are a man of sense. I do not receive money, you understand, on my own account, but for the sake of the giver. One squanders, you observe, and another saves. Now I hold it fitting, that I the master should catch, and that the scholar be the man to cast away.

BUYER.

I thought you had just declared the contrary. Did not you say, that the youth was the person to get carefully, and that you yourself, who alone can be rich, were the person to give liberally?

CHRYSIPPUS.

What, you are witty then! Take heed, that I do not shoot you with an indefinite syllogism!

BUYER.

Why should I be afraid of such a weapon as that?

CHRYSIPPUS.

Why afraid? The effect of it would be doubt, and silence, and distraction, nothing less.

More

More than that, if I were so disposed, I could even petrify you in an instant, making you plainly appear to be a stone.

BUYER.

A stone! my good Sir, I do not take you to be a [*p*] Perseus.

CHRYSIPPUS.

Do you only mind what I say to you. Is not a stone a body?

BUYER.

Yes.

CHRYSIPPUS.

And is not an animal a body?

BUYER.

Yes.

CHRYSIPPUS.

And are not you an animal?

BUYER.

I suppose so.

[*p*] Perseus, having attacked Medusa when her snakes were asleep, cut off her head, and set it on his ægis, whence he derived the faculty of turning men into stones.

CHRYSIPPUS.

Then you are a stone, Sir, as being a body.

BUYER.

I do not desire to be any such thing. I beg you will make me proper amends for this usage, and let me be a man again.

CHRYSIPPUS.

You shall be a man again: there is no difficulty in that. Whatever is body is animal. Is it not?

BUYER.

No.

CHRYSIPPUS.

Is a stone an animal?

BUYER.

No.

CHRYSIPPUS.

Are you a body?

BUYER.

Yes.

CHRYSIPPUS.

And being a body, you are an animal.

BUYER.

BUYER.

True.

CHRYSIPPUS.

Then, being an animal, you are not a stone.

BUYER.

Upon my word I am very much obliged to you. It is entirely owing to your goodness, that my limbs are not as cold and as stiff as those of Niobe. I will buy you. Mercury, what do you ask for this gentleman?

MERCURY.

[q] Twelve minæ.

BUYER.

Here, take the money.

MERCURY.

Pray do you buy him solely on your own account?

BUYER.

No, I do not. Do not you see all these people?

[q] Thirty-eight pounds, fifteen shillings.

MER-

MERCURY.

I see a number of broad shoulders, very fit to elucidate the [r] Reaper.

JUPITER.

Come, do not let us lose our time. Call another.

MERCURY.

Now for the [s] peripatetick, the handsome, the rich.—What do you say to him, Gentlemen? He is exceedingly wise, he understands every thing.

BUYER.

How do you describe him?

MERCURY.

Moderate, gentle, fit for the world. What is best of all, he is double.

BUYER.

What?

MERCURY.

He is one thing within, another thing without. You must remember, if you purchase

---

[r] A pun on the species of argumentation, called, ὁ θερίζων, the Reaper.

[s] Aristotle.

him, that you are to call this internal, that external.

BUYER.

What does he profess?

MERCURY.

He professes that good things are three-fold, in the soul, and in the body, and in neither the one nor the other.

BUYER.

A good sensible kind of a man! Pray what is the price of him?

MERCURY.

[t] Twenty minæ.

BUYER.

You rate him very high, upon my word.

MERCURY.

Indeed I do not. You will find your account in him, and I would not advise you to delay the purchase a moment. Consider, Sir, what a stock of knowledge you will immediately lay in. He will teach you how long a gnat may live, how deep the rays of the sun penetrate

[t] Sixty-four pounds, eleven shillings, and eight-pence.

into the sea, and what sort of a soul an oyster has.

BUYER.

All that shews great accuracy of investigation.

MERCURY.

But all that is nothing. For you would be astonished, were you to hear a few instances, that might be mentioned, of his discernment. O that you could but once hear him discourse on production, on generation, on the formation of embryos! He would prove to you, Sir, that man is a risible animal, and that an [u] ass is neither made for laughing, nor building, nor sailing.

BUYER.

His precepts are most respectable and important! I will give you the twenty minæ for him.

MERCURY.

Very well. Who remains yet unsold? Oh! there is Pyrrho, the sceptick. Come hither, Sir, that you may be put up without further loss of time. The company is going away, and

[u] This opinion, Bourdelotius tells us, is not universally received, an author of his acquaintance having maintained the contrary.

there are very few bidders. Who will give any thing for him?

BUYER.

I will. Only I should be glad to ask him beforehand what he knows.

PHILOSOPHER.

Nothing.

BUYER.

What do you mean?

PHILOSOPHER.

I mean that, as far as I can see, there is nothing that has any being.

BUYER.

Then you and I, I suppose, are nothing at all?

PHILOSOPHER.

I cannot say.

BUYER.

You yourself you suppose to be something?

PHILOSOPHER.

That is a matter, of which I am more ignorant still.

BUYER.

This is doubting with a witness. But what do you do with these scales?

PHILOSOPHER.

In thefe fcales I ponder arguments, till I make them of equal weight. When I fee them thus reduced to perfect equality, then it becomes impoffible for me, you know, to prefer one to another.

BUYER.

And with regard to other matters, is there any thing in which you may be depended on?

PHILOSOPHER.

Yes; you may rely on me in every thing elfe except in purfuing a fugitive.

BUYER.

Why not in that too?

PHILOSOPHER.

The reafon is, Sir, I cannot [*x*] apprehend.

[*x*] It will readily be *apprehended*, that the wit of this paffage is merely a pun arifing from a technical term. The fcepticks maintained, that the human mind was incapable fully to comprehend or lay hold of any propofition whatever in all its parts. Hence their ακαταληψια, incomprehenfibility. The word *apprehend* in the tranflation is preferred to *comprehend*, on account of its double meaning, being applicable both to body and mind.

BUYER.

I believe you: you seem to be slow and heavy enough in all conscience. And pray to what does your knowledge tend?

PHILOSOPHER.

To ignorance, to be both blind and dumb.

BUYER.

And can you neither hear nor see?

PHILOSOPHER.

Not only so, but I am no better than a reptile, that is without sense and judgment.

BUYER.

Truly these are great recommendations! I must have you. What price do you put upon him.

MERCURY.

An [y] Attick mina.

BUYER.

Take it. Well, Sir, what do you say to me now? Have not I bought you?

[y] Three pounds, four shillings, and seven-pence.

PHILOSOPHER.

It is quite uncertain.

BUYER.

Uncertain! How can it be uncertain? I have not only bought you, but paid for you.

PHILOSOPHER.

It is not a matter to be haſtily determined: I muſt deliberate and conſider the ſubject in every point of view.

BUYER.

Deliberate! Come along with me, I tell you, as you ought to do. I have bought you, and you are mine.

PHILOSOPHER.

Who can tell whether what you ſay be true?

BUYER.

The auctioneer knows it to be true. All the company ſaw me give him the mina.

PHILOSOPHER.

Is there any company here then?

BUYER.

I believe I shall fully satisfy you, without more ado, when you come to grind in my mill, that I am your master: you will then have somewhat the [z] worse of the argument.

PHILOSOPHER.

I suspend my determination.

BUYER.

But so do not I, for I have declared mine openly.

MERCURY.

Come, come, leave off this silly opposition, and go along with your master. — To-morrow, Gentlemen, we shall be glad to see you again. We shall then have a variety of lots to dispose of, consisting of private persons, pedlars, and mechanicks.

[z] τινων κατα τον χειρω λογον. Arisloph. Νεφ. ΙΙΙ. 2. λεγε; οτλον και ηριτλον.

[a] MINOS AND SOSTRATUS.

MINOS.

LET the robber Sostratus be tossed into [b] Pyriphlegethon. And let him, who has been convicted of sacrilege, be torn in pieces by the [c] chimæra. But as for the tyrant, let him be stretched at his length by the side of [d] Tityus, that his liver also may be gnawed by the vultures. Those who have been good are immediately to repair to the plains of Elysium, and to take up their abode in the isles of

---

[a] A dialogue of the dead. Minos was a king of Crete, in which station, having behaved well, he was, after he became a subject of Pluto, appointed lord chief justice of the king's bench. See Virg. Æn. VI. 432.

[b] One of the infernal rivers. Its name is derived from πυρ fire, and φλεγω to burn.

[c] A dreadful monster, with which few readers are unacquainted.

"Gorgons, and Hydras, and Chimæras dire."
Par. Lost. b. II. v. 628.

[d] Tityus behaved very rudely to Latona, for which Jupiter knocked him down with his thunderbolt. He was afterwards sentenced to feed vultures with his entrails, which grew as fast as they were devoured. His body covered nine acres.

the

the blessed, in return for the benefits they have conferred on mankind.

SOSTRATUS.

I beg and beseech of you, Minos, only to hear me speak, and then judge whether what I say be reasonable.

MINOS.

Have not I heard you already? You have been a wicked villain. You have several times committed murder, and have been fairly tried and convicted.

SOSTRATUS.

I do not pretend to deny what has been fully proved against me. But the justice of my punishment is what I would beg leave to submit to your consideration.

MINOS:

The justice of your punishment! How can it be otherwise than just? Is any thing more just than to punish wickedness?

SOSTRATUS.

I only crave your indulgence to answer me a question or two. I promise not to detain you long.

MINOS.

MINOS.

Well, do not be tedious then: I must go on with the trials of the rest.

SOSTRATUS.

Tell me, I pray, did the actions of my life proceed from my own voluntary motion, or were they ordained by fate?

MINOS.

Ordained by fate. That is clear enough.

SOSTRATUS.

How then can either the good or the bad be more than seemingly so, since whatever they do is done merely in subserviency to fate?

MINOS.

Why, yes, to be sure, Clotho does allot to every man that is born what he is to do in his life.

SOSTRATUS.

If then a person, subject to the will of another, should be obliged to commit a murder—suppose, for instance, an executioner, or a soldier, in obedience to the orders of a judge, or a tyrant—whom would you charge with the guilt?

MINOS.

MINOS.

The judge, or the tyrant, without all doubt. I should blame the efficient cause, not the [e] instrument that is used.

SOSTRA-

[e] The Athenians had a festival, called, Διιπολια, from Jupiter Polleus, and Βυφονια, from killing an ox. In this festival it was the custom to place certain cakes, of the same sort with those used at sacrifices, upon a table of brass; round this they drove a select number of oxen, of which he that eat any of the cakes was presently slaughtered. The person that killed the ox was called Βυλας, or Βυφονος. Porphyry reports, that no less than three families were employed in this ceremony, and received different names from their offices therein: the family, whose duty it was to drive the oxen, were called κεντριαδαι, from κεντρον, a spur: those that knocked him down, Βυττοι, being descended from Thaulon: those that slaughtered and cut him up, δαιτροι, butchers, or cooks. The original of the custom was thus: On one of Jupiter's festivals, it happened, that a hungry ox eat one of the consecrated cakes; whereupon the priest (some call him Thaulon, others Domus, or Sopater), moved with a pious zeal, killed the profane beast. In those days it was looked upon as a capital crime to kill an ox; wherefore the guilty priest was forced to secure himself by a timely flight; and the Athenians in his stead took the bloody ax, arraigned it, and, according to Pausanias, brought it in not guilty. But Ælian is of another opinion, and reports, that the priest and people present at the solemnity (for they also were accused as being accessary to the fact) were acquitted, but the ax condemned, which

seems

SOSTRATUS.

I thank you, Minos, for your candour, and for this illustration of the argument. Very well, Sir; and if a servant, by command of his master, brings you money, to whom do you think yourself indebted? Which of the two is to be considered as your benefactor?

MINOS.

The sender, and not the bringer, who only did as he was bidden.

SOSTRATUS.

Do not you see then how cruel and unjust it is in you to punish us, who are merely servants and ministers to execute the orders of Clotho? And is it not equally absurd to honour and reward those benefactors to mankind, who have generously bestowed what never was their own? For I defy any one to alledge, that there can ever be a possibility of refusing to comply with the appointments of necessity.

---

seems to be the most probable. In memory of these actions, it became ever after customary for the priest to fly, and judgment to be given about the slaughter of the ox.

Potter's Antiq.

MINOS.

MINOS.

Since you are so nice an examiner, Sostratus, you may chance to discover many other things not altogether so agreeable to reason. And you will obtain this by your enquiries, that you will be looked upon in the double capacity of a robber and a sophist.—Mercury set this man free, and let us hear no more complaints of his punishment.—But hark you, Sostratus; do not you go and teach other dead men to ask impertinent questions, and to be as saucy as yourself.

AJAX AND AGAMEMNON.
AGAMEMNON.

IF you, Ajax, in your madness, not only shed your own blood, but would most gladly have murdered every man of us, how can you pretend to find fault with Ulysses? You would not so much as vouchsafe to speak to your old friend and fellow-soldier, nor even to look at him, when he lately came to consult the prophet, but proudly and sternly stalked [f] away.

[f] See Hom. Od. II.
" Stern as Ajax' spectre stalk'd away."
Pope's Dunciad, b. IV. speaking of Dr. Bentley.

AJAX.

AJAX.

I had reason, Agamemnon, for what I did. My madness was entirely owing to him; it was he alone who contended with me for the arms.

AGAMEMNON.

What, did you expect to meet with no opposition, but to prevail over every body without any manner of trouble?

AJAX.

In that matter I did. Achilles was my [g] cousin, and his arms were no more than my right. Were not you, all of you, though greatly his superiors, contented to give up this point in my favour? How could the son of Laertes, whom I had so often saved from being knocked on the head by the Trojans—how could he presume to think himself preferable to me, and better entitled to my cousin's arms?

AGAMEMNON.

You must blame Thetis, my dear Sir; if, when it was her business to secure to you the inheritance of the arms, as being a relation,

---

[g] Ajax was the son of Telamon, who was the brother of Peleus, the father of Achilles.

she

she thought proper to wave all that, and [*b*] refer your respective claims to a publick decision.

AJAX.

I have nothing to say against her. I can blame nobody but Ulysses; he was my only competitor.

AGAMEMNON.

And you should forgive him, if he was; since it was so very natural for him to be borne away with the love of glory, a thing so desired by us all, for which we are all of us so contented to encounter dangers, and which had so great an influence over you yourself, in the opinion of the [*i*] Trojan arbitrators.

AJAX.

I know very well who was the undoing of me. But one must not presume to say any thing con-

---

[*b*] Ὄνκεν πόλιας μήτης. Hom. Od. Λ. 544.

[*i*] We are told by a scholiast on the above quotation from Homer, that Agamemnon, to avoid all suspicion of partiality in the affair of the arms, asked of the Trojan captives, which of the two claimants, Ajax or Ulysses, had done them more mischief; when they immediately answered, Ulysses,

cerning

cerning the [*k*] celestials. However, there is one thing, Agamemnon, which the goddess herself shall not make me do: Minerva herself shall never hinder me from hating him.

DIOGENES, ANTISTHENES, CRATES.

DIOGENES.

SINCE we have nothing else to do, Gentlemen, suppose we take a walk to the entrance of these regions, and see who are coming down to us, and how they behave?

ANTISTHENES.

With all my heart, Diogenes; let us go. It will be some amusement to us to see them weeping and wailing, and intreating Mercury to let them go. We shall find some of them most reluctantly submitting to be dragged on neck and heels, pitching their feet against the ground, and making all the resistance they can, though to no manner of purpose.

[*k*] Meaning Minerva, or Wisdom, who could not, as Eustathius observes, but prefer Ulysses to Ajax, as more resembling herself.

" Παφλις δι Τρως διασως και Παλλας Αθηη." Od. A. 546.

CRATES.

CRATES.

Shall I tell you what fell under my obferva-
tion in my way down hither?

DIOGENES.

Pray do: I fuppofe fomething very entertaining.

CRATES.

There were a great many in company, and,
amongſt others, feveral perfons of diſtinction.
There was my rich [*l*] countryman Iſmenodorus; Arſaces, the governour of Media; and
Orœtes, the Armenian. Iſmenodorus had been
murdered by fome robbers on mount Cithæron,
as he was going to Eleufis. He put his two
hands to the place where he had received his
death's wound, and groaned moſt piteouſly.
He often called on his young children, which
he had thus been obliged to leave behind him,
and greatly blamed himſelf for his raſhnefs, in
venturing to paſs over Cithæron and the parts
about Eleutherӕ, places fo waſted by the wars,
while he was accompanied with only two fer-

[*l*] A Theban.

vants:

vants; and this at a time when he carried with him five golden beakers, besides four other large drinking cups. Arsaces, though considerably advanced in years, was far from being an ill-looking man. But he stormed like any barbarian. He could not bear the thoughts of [m] walking on foot, calling out lustily for a horse to be brought him. For the very same wound, you are to know, had dispatched both his horse and himself. This wound was given him by a Thracian soldier, in the engagement with the Cappadocians, near the river Araxes. Arsaces had advanced with great eagerness, as he said, far before his attendants. The Thracian, stooping to receive Arsaces on his buckler, disarmed him, and, at the very same instant,

[m] It was reckoned an infamous thing amongst the Medes and Persians for one of their great men to be seen walking on foot. To descend to every vice was not more a disgrace than to be dismounted from his horse. See Xenophon. Cyrop. and Justin. de Parthis. XLI. 3. These eastern gentry dispatched every kind of business, publick and private, eat and drank, and in short did every thing, on horseback. This was what distinguished the free men from the slaves, the latter being obliged to go on foot, which was a mode of progression in which their masters scorned to budge an inch.

run both horse and rider through their bodies
with his long spear.

ANTISTHENES.

Pray, was it possible to be done at one stroke?

CRATES.

[n] Yes, very possible. While he rushed
on, extending his pike twenty cubits in length,
the Thracian, evading the point, beat off the
force of it with his buckler. Falling on his
knee he receives the charge with his spear,
meanwhile the horse, being struck on the breast,
is stabbed by his own vehemence and spirit.
At the same time the spear, entering at the
groin, goes quite through the body of Arsaces.
Now you see it was easy enough to be done,
being not so much the action of the man, as of
the horse. The gentleman was highly offended
to see himself no better accommodated in his
way hither than an ordinary person, thinking it
very hard that he could not have a horse to ride
upon. Orœtes too, though a private man, was

[a] Consuetudine sua ad pedes desilierunt: suffossisque
equis, compluribusque nostris disjectis, reliquos in fugam
conjecerunt. Cæsar's Com. iv. 9.

nevertheless extremely delicate and tender in his feet, being hardly able to walk, or even to stand. This is the case with the Medes in general: if they have parted with their horses, they cannot [o] proceed any farther without the greatest difficulty, going on their tip-toes, as if they trod upon thorns. Orœtes threw himself all along upon the ground, and could not by any means be prevailed on to get up. Upon this, honest Mercury was fain to hoist him upon his back, and so carry him to the boat. I laughed.

ANTISTHENES.

When I came down I did not think of mixing with the crowd, but left my companions to lament at their leisure, running before them to the boat, to secure myself a good place. I own I was not a little delighted during the voyage: there was a good deal of weeping, and a good deal of vomiting.

[o] Hippocrates takes notice of the bad consequences arising from being continually on horseback. Hippoc. περι ιππων, υδατων, τοπων. All sedentary persons must be sensible of the bad consequences of being very seldom on horseback.

DIOGENES.

So much for your fellow-travellers. Mine were Blepsias, the usurer of Piræeus; Lampis of Acharnæ, general of the mercenaries; and the rich Damis of Corinth. Damis had been poisoned by his son. Lampis had dispatched himself for the love of Myrtium the harlot. And poor Blepsias was reported to have died of want; of which indeed he exhibited all the appearance, being pale and thin to the very last degree. I had a fancy to ask them the occasion of their dying, notwithstanding I had already been told, being curious to hear what they could have to say. And while Damis was accusing his son, "How could you reasonably expect any thing better of him?" said I, you an old fellow of ninety, and worth a thousand talents, to grudge a youth of eighteen a few sorry oboli, while you yourself roll in all manner of luxury!" "And you, Mr. Acharnian," said I (while he was sighing, and groaning, and swearing, by turns) "what do you think of yourself? Why do you pretend to complain of the tyranny of love? And not rather blame yourself? You did not use to be dismayed by an enemy, but were the

foremost to rush on danger. And for such a
stout fellow as you to suffer yourself to become
the whining captive of a poor ordinary wench,
armed only with sighs and a few feigned tears—
O for shame!" As to Blepsias, he had sense of
himself to recollect what a fool he had been, in
not enjoying his wealth when he might; which,
as he could not live for ever, he lamented the
necessity of being obliged to leave to persons
no way related to him. And now I had the
great pleasure of enjoying a general groan.
But behold! we have got to the entrance. Let
us see who are coming yonder. Wonderful!
what a swarm of all sorts of people, and every
one in tears, excepting only children, and babes
newly born! The very oldest of them all are
full of lamentation! What can be the meaning
of it? There must be something of fascination
surely in this business, which makes them so
passionately fond of life! But I will put the
question to this decrepit old fellow. What can
you thus weep for at this time of day, old boy?
A person of your age and experience, one would
think, might be contented to die without
grumbling. Pray what were you? A king
perhaps?

POOR MAN.

A king! say you? No, not I, indeed.

DIOGENES.

A lord?

POOR MAN.

Not I.

DIOGENES.

You muſt have been very rich. You muſt ſurely have fared moſt deliciouſly in life; or you could not be ſo mortified at the thoughts of leaving it.

POOR MAN.

No ſuch thing, I tell you. I was near ninety years of age, and lived in great poverty. My utmoſt induſtry in my wretched employment of a fiſherman was barely ſufficient to keep ſoul and body together. No man's circumſtances could be more miſerable than mine. I had no child to comfort me. I was very lame, and almoſt blind.

DIOGENES.

And could you, notwithſtanding all this, ſtill cheriſh a deſire to live?

POOR MAN.

Yes; the light was still sweet; and death was something very dreadful, which I could not but wish to escape.

DIOGENES.

You trifle at a strange rate, old man, and run counter to all reason and order. Fie for shame! A man, contemporary with Charon, to be such a child! One needs not so much to wonder at the folly of youth, when old age itself can be thus ridiculous! old age, which might reasonably be expected to long for death, the only remedy of its numerous evils!—But let us take ourselves away from this place, lest we too should be suspected of the folly of meditating an escape.

MENIPPUS AND CHIRON.

MENIPPUS.

I HAVE been told, Chiron, that you, though a god, were desirous of dying.

CHIRON.

CHIRON.

You have been told no more than was true, Menippus. I might have continued immortal; but, you see, I [*p*] chose to die.

MENIPPUS.

What strange passion, I wonder, for death could so unaccountably possess you; which is so very little desirable to the generality of mankind?

CHIRON.

As you are a man of sense, I will tell you. I had no longer any pleasure to enjoy in immortality.

MENIPPUS.

No! was it not a most delightful thing to live and [*q*] behold the light?

[*p*] Chiron was the son of Saturn and Philyra. He was wounded by Hercules in the foot, with an arrow dipped in the blood of the Hydra; which put him to such exquisite pain, that Jupiter, in compassion to him, turned him into Sagittarius, one of the twelve signs.

[*q*] To behold the light. A favourite saying of Euripides, often repeated by Lucian.

CHIRON.

CHIRON.

No, Menippus. Pleasure, in my opinion, consists in novelty and variety; whereas human life is nothing more than merely a repetition of always the same over and over again. I grew sick of such a perpetual round, the same sun, the same light, the same eating and drinking, the same seasons, the same every thing, revolving in constant succession. That which is always one and the same can never be pleasure: pleasure must be a participation of whatever is new and unexpected.

MENIPPUS.

Well, Sir. And how do you find matters here below? In this your chosen residence, it is to be hoped, you find things more to your mind.

CHIRON.

I assure you, Menippus, I think my situation here far from being unpleasant. This universal equality is a thing very taking; whether you are conspicuous or obscure, it makes no difference. And then hunger and thirst are sensations unknown here; the good things above are nothing to us, we want them not.

MENIPPUS.

But I pray, Sir, does not this panegyrick of yours speak the same language as the censure with which you set out? And are you not now contradicting your own doctrine?

CHIRON.

How?

MENIPPUS.

If you grew tired of life, because it was nothing more than always the same thing over and over again, you must for that very reason soon be weary of your situation here, and wish to change it for another life; which, I believe, you will find to be impossible.

CHIRON.

What can a body do, Menippus?

MENIPPUS.

A man of sense, I think, will act as is commonly advised. He will endeavour to rest contented, and make the most of his present condition, allowing every individual circumstance of it to be very tolerable.

NIREUS.

NIREUS, THERSITES, MENIPPUS.

NIREUS.

HERE is Menippus, who will determine the question between us. Menippus, do not you think, that I am handsomer than he is?

MENIPPUS.

But who are you? first let me know that.

NIREUS.

[r] Nireus and Thersites.

MENIPPUS.

Still I am ignorant which of you is Nireus, and which Thersites: that does not appear.

THERSITES.

One thing appears very plainly, that I have the honour of being very like Nireus, and that there is not the difference between us, which Homer's blindness induced him to believe there was. Homer has described him as the handsomest of men. But, in the opinion of altogether as good a [s] judge, there was nothing

[r] Nireus names himself first, to *back* his opinion.
[s] Minos.

so much amiss in a few straggling hairs scattered over a sugar-loaf head, as to make me at all his inferior. What do you say, Menippus? Look at us both, and then determine.

NIREUS.

Determine! sayest thou; a very pretty question!

"Niréus [1], whom Aglac to Charopus bore,
"Nireus of faultless form and fairest face,
"The loveliest youth of all the Grecian race."

MENIPPUS.

At Troy you might be the loveliest of all the Grecian race; I do not deny it. But here the case is different. Bones here are bones, bare bones, and nothing more. The only difference between your fine skull and that of Thersites is, that yours is more liable to be cracked; it is so soft, and has so little of the man in it.

NIREUS.

Only be so good as to ask Homer what a figure I made in the Grecian camp.

[1] Hom. Il. II. 671.

MENIPPUS.

Do not tell me of Homer. Those who were with you in the Grecian camp may give whatever account they please. I have the perfect use of my own eyes, and can see very well what you are at present.

NIREUS.

And so, Sir, I am no handsomer than he is?

MENIPPUS.

How can any body be said to be handsome here, where all are exactly alike?

THERSITES.

Now I am satisfied. That is all I desire.

✶✶✶✶✶✶

DIOGENES, MAUSOLUS.

DIOGENES.

PRAY, [*u*] Mr. Carian, what pretence have you for carrying your head so high above every body else?

[*u*] The original is ω καρ, ιτι τιιι μιγα φρονις; a very good motto for any body inclined to censure this translation.

MAUSOLUS.

Pretence! Becaufe, Mr. Sinopian, I have been a king. I ruled over all Caria, and a confiderable part of Lydia. I fubdued feveral iflands, and conquered the greateft part of Ionia, advancing as far as Miletus.— Befides my being great and mighty in war, I was very handfome. But, not to infift on this, I have the honour of repofing under a fuperb monument at Halicarnaffus, of fo ftupendous a fize, and of fo high a polifh, that no other man was ever kept under by any thing fo fine. The horfes and men are carved to fuch a degree of perfection, and in fuch exquifite marble, as you could not eafily match even in a [x] temple. And do not you think I have reafon to be proud?

[x] The ancients were wont to difregard their own houfes in comparifon of the publick buildings. "Italiam ornare, "quàm domum fuam, illi maluerunt." The monument of Maufolus was called Maufoleum, and reckoned amongft the wonders of the world. His wife Artemifia concluded with making for him this fuperb monument, after having begun with drinking up his afhes.

DIOGENES.

What, becauſe you have been a king, and becauſe your monument is ſo well poliſhed and ſo very heavy?

MAUSOLUS.

Yes.

DIOGENES.

But conſider, dread Sir. As fine a fellow as you were, your beauty and ſtrength too are both gone at preſent. Were we to refer the matter to an arbitration, I believe, no reaſon would appear why your ſkull ſhould be deemed preferable to mine. For both are equally bald and naked. We both of us ſhew our teeth in juſt the ſame manner. We are equally deprived of our eyes. Our noſes are flattened alike. The people of Halicarnaſſus indeed may value themſelves on ſuch magnificence, and may boaſt of the precious ſtones which compoſe your monument, which no doubt they will puff off to ſtrangers, and ſhew as a mighty fine thing. But, as for you, I cannot ſee what great advantage you can derive from it, unleſs you find it convenient to be under a great heap of huge ſtones, and carry a heavier load than any body elſe.

MAUSOLUS.

And muſt all go for nothing then? And is Mauſolus to be no better accounted of than Diogenes?

DIOGENES.

No better? no; not ſo well. Mauſolus will not fail to lament moſt bitterly, when he remembers the good things upon earth, in which he placed his happineſs. Mean while, Diogenes will laugh at him. Mauſolus will conſtantly talk of his monument in Halicarnaſſus, built by his wife and ſiſter; while Diogenes neither knows nor cares whether he has any monument at all. Having lived more like a man, Diogenes leaves behind him a reputation, which all thoſe, whoſe opinions are worth regarding, will think ſomething better worth talking of than the monument of a wretched Carian king, as having a much more ſolid foundation.

※※※※※

CHARON, MENIPPUS, MERCURY.

CHARON.

PAY me my fare, I ſay. You raſcal, pay me my fare.

MENIPPUS.

O if you like bawling, Charon, by all means bawl.

CHARON.

I say, pay me for bringing you over.

MENIPPUS.

Do you expect to receive money, whether a passenger has it or no?

CHARON.

Has it or no! Pray who is there so poor, that he cannot advance an obolus?

MENIPPUS.

I do not pretend to know how it may be with other people, but I hope I may speak for myself; I tell you, I have not one.

CHARON.

You dog, pay me immediately, or I will throttle you.

MENIPPUS.

Say another word, and I will lay my staff over your head.

CHARON.

CHARON.

And so you think to sail all this way for nothing?

MENIPPUS.

Was I not given up to your care by Mercury? Mercury is answerable for me.

MERCURY.

Upon my word, I am likely to have a fine time of it, if I am to be accountable for every man that dies!

CHARON.

I will not quit you. You shall not get off so, believe me.

MENIPPUS.

Here you may flay, that is certain, and keep dunning me for your fare! But how can you reasonably hope to receive what a body has not to give?

CHARON.

Then you ought to have brought money with you.

MENIPPUS.

I knew that very well; but I tell you I had none to bring. Cannot a man die without having money?

CHARON.

CHARON.

You are the only paſſenger who ſhall boaſt of my bringing you over the river for [y] nothing.

MENIPPUS.

For nothing! pray, my good Sir, recollect yourſelf a little. Did I not both pump and row for you? And was I not the only paſſenger you had, who did not trouble you with tears?

CHARON.

All this fine talk does not pay me my fare. You ſhould indeed give me an obolus. It is no more than my due, and I ought to have it.

MENIPPUS.

If you cannot make yourſelf eaſy without it, you had better row me back again.

CHARON.

Yes, to be ſure! that I may put Æacus in a paſſion, and get myſelf a good beating!

[y] Whatever airs Charon may give himſelf, very reputable authors aſſert, that all perſons who had lived in the neighbourhood of the lake Avernus, as well as many others, were free of his boat, and under no obligation to bring him their Δανακη, or obolus.   Strabo and others.

MENIPPUS.

Then behave yourself better, and do not be troublesome.

CHARON.

Let me see what you have in your wallet.

MENIPPUS.

You are very welcome. I have nothing in it except some lupines and Hecate's supper.

CHARON.

Where could you find such a cynick, Mercury? At what a rate his tongue has gone during the whole voyage! He has been laughing and scoffing at all the rest of the passengers. While they wept without ceasing, he alone continued singing.

MERCURY.

By what I can find, Charon, you do not seem to know who he is that you have had in your boat. It is Menippus, Sir, and no other. Freedom of speech is his motto; he cares for nobody.

CHARON.

Let me but have him once more.

MENIPPUS.

Once more! do you say? Do not flatter yourself. You will not catch me a second time.

※※※

PLUTO AND PROTESILAUS.

PROTESILAUS.

MY lord, my king, my supreme, and you, O daughter of Ceres, I beg of you both not to despise a lover's petition.

PLUTO.

What do you want? Who are you?

PROTESILAUS.

I am Protesilaus, at your service, the son of Iphiclus of Phylace. I accompanied the Greeks in their expedition against Troy, and there I was killed the very first man. My request is, that you would be so good as to let me return to life for a little while.

PLUTO.

You are not singular in your love of life. It is the universal passion of the dead, an object which no one of them must ever enjoy!

PROTESILAUS.

It is not merely for the fake of living, Pluto, but on account of my wife, that I am so earnest to go back. I had but just had time to marry her, when I was obliged to leave her, and set sail. And, wretch as I was! I was no sooner got to land, than I was slain by Hector. I do assure you, Pluto, I can have no rest for the love of her. Suffer me only to pay her a visit. I will return directly.

PLUTO.

You have not had your draught of Lethe, I suppose?

PROTESILAUS.

Yes, I have. But this love, Sir, this love still prevails.

PLUTO.

But why cannot you have patience. Your wife will come hither to you by and by: there can be no manner of necessity for you to go to her.

PROTESILAUS.

You talk of patience, Pluto. I tell you, Sir, it is impossible to have patience. As you have

have been in love yourself, you might be expected to know something of the matter.

PLUTO.

But what mighty business could it be to live again for one short day, when you would soon be as miserable again as ever?

PROTESILAUS.

I am of opinion that I could persuade her to [z] follow me down hither. In which case, you know, you would be able to add two instead of one to the number of the dead.

PLUTO.

Such a thing has never been, and it is not fit it should.

PROTESILAUS.

I beg your pardon; I can mention you more precedents than one. Pray, what was your reason for delivering up Eurydice to Orpheus? And did not you grant my [a] cousin Alcestis leave of absence, purely to please Hercules?

PLUTO.

[z] Laodamia actually hanged herself, they say, in order to have her husband's company.

[a] If the reader wishes to know the exact degree of consanguinity between Protesilaus and Alcestis, here it is, as recorded

PLUTO.

And you would go and expose that bare skull of yours in all its uglinefs to a fine young bride! How do you expect her to receive you, when she could not so much as know you? I am very sure she would run away from you in a fright, and you must be contented to have your labour for your pains.

PROSERPINE.

True, husband; but it is in your power to provide a remedy against that. Why cannot you order Mercury, as foon as Protefilaus is landed in day-light, to give him a reftorative touch with his rod, and make him as young and as handfome as the moment he left her?

PLUTO.

You muft take this man back again, Mercury, fince my wife will have it so, and make

corded by the Guillims of ancient days:

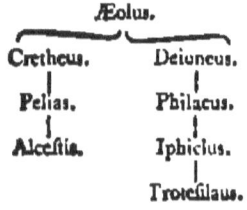

him

him a bridegroom. — But remember, Sir! — only a single day!

MENIPPUS AND CERBERUS.

MENIPPUS.

AS you are a brother cynick, I hope, Cerberus, you will oblige me by answering a question. For being a [b] god, I presume you are not only capable of barking, but talking too, whenever you think fit. I want very much to know how Socrates behaved himself in his descent to these regions.

CERBERUS.

While he was at a considerable distance, he advanced with a firm step and [c] steady countenance, as if quite fearless of death, and de-

---

[b] Cerberus is not a little obliged to Lucian for the honourable title which he here gives him, hardly any body else having been so complaisant to him.   Hemsterhusius.

[c] Socrates was so remarkable for maintaining a steady countenance, that even the scolding of his wife made little or no impression upon it. Ciceronis Tusc. qu. 3, 31. In which respect that admirable philosopher remains to this day without a rival. October 26, 1778.

sirous

sirous of shewing his fortitude to those that stood by. But, when once he had got within the chasm, and saw how dismally dark it was, he began to be staggered. And especially when I snapped at him with my [d] hemlock, and laid hold of his leg, he wept like an infant. He bewailed the loss of his children; and could not tell which way to turn himself.

MENIPPUS.

Was Socrates then a mere sophist? And did he not in reality look with contempt on death?

CERBERUS.

No such thing, I tell you. Indeed, after being convinced how absolutely necessary it was to submit, he assumed an air of unconcern. When he saw there was no possibility of being excused, he wisely determined to set a good face on the matter; that he might at least be somewhat admired, if he could obtain nothing more.

[d] The meaning of this passage is gathered from Pliny's Nat. Hist. 27, 2. who informs us, that Aconite, the most expeditious of all poisons, was produced from the foam of Cerberus, as Hercules was dragging him from hell, and that it grows about Heraclea Pontica, which, it seems, is on that road.

I have

I have always obferved of fuch fort of people, that, till they come to the entrance, they are perfect heroes; but behold! they are the next moment the arranteft cowards in nature.

MENIPPUS.

Pray, what did you think of my behaviour, when I came down?

CERBERUS.

I can fay of you, Menippus, and of Diogenes before you, that you acted in a manner worthy of the [*e*] family. To you two alone there was no need of any compulfion to pufh you on. You entered volunteers, laughing at your companions, and advifing them by no means to neglect weeping and wailing.

MENIPPUS, ÆACUS, PYTHAGORAS, EMPEDOCLES, AND SOCRATES.

MENIPPUS.

FOR Pluto's fake, Æacus, be fo good as to fhew me whatever is to be feen here in hell.

[*e*] Of cynicks.

ÆACUS.

ÆACUS.

It would not be so easy a matter, Menippus, to shew you all: but I can give you some general information concerning the principal things. This, you know, is Cerberus; and, I dare say, you have not forgotten the old ferryman, who brought you over. You saw the lake and Pyriphlegethon at your first entrance.

MENIPPUS.

Yes, yes, I remember all these very well. And I know you; you are porter here. I have seen the king too, and the furies. But I very much long to have a look at the men of antiquity, and especially such as have distinguished themselves.

ÆACUS.

Very well, Sir. This gentleman is Agamemnon. That is Achilles. Next to him is Idomeneus, then Ulysses, then Ajax, then Diomede, and the rest of the celebrated Greeks all in a row.

MENIPPUS.

And is such, alas! old Homer, the end of thy heroes! And do the chief honours of thy poem

poem thus perish unknown! Dust and vanity! Mere [*f*] visionary personages without shape and substance! — But pray, Æacus, who may this be?

ÆACUS.

Cyrus. And that is Crœsus. Close by him stands Sardanapalus. Somewhat higher up is Midas. And behold! there is Xerxes.

MENIPPUS.

Xerxes indeed! It was you, you rascal, who made all Greece to tremble. Nothing less would serve you than making a bridge over the Hellespont, and sailing over the tops of mountains! Crœsus too, I think, does not make so great a figure at present. Here is Sardanapalus: I hope, Æacus, you will permit me just to give him one good slap on the chops.

ÆACUS.

By no means. Why, you would beat his head to pieces: it was not made to bear blows.

MENIPPUS.

At least I may spit in his face: he is not too delicate for such a salute as that.

[*f*] ομηρα καπνα. Hom. Od. A. 251.

ÆACUS.

ÆACUS.

Have you a mind that I should shew you the wise men?

MENIPPUS.

If you please, I shall be obliged to you?

ÆACUS.

The first is Pythagoras.

MENIPPUS.

Your most humble servant, Euphorbus, or Apollo, or whatever other character you choose to appear in, I am very glad to see you.

PYTHAGORAS.

Sir, your servant.

MENIPPUS.

Pray, Sir, what is become of your golden thigh?

PYTHAGORAS.

O that is neither here nor there; I had rather talk of something to eat. Pray, what have you got in your wallet?

MENIPPUS.

My wallet has nothing in it but a few beans, and consequently nothing fit for Pythagoras to eat.

PYTHAGORAS.

Only give me some, and let me try. Since I have been here I have learned a new leſſon. I do not now infiſt upon it, that a bean and the head of a parent are quite the ſame thing.

ÆACUS.

This is Solon, the ſon of Execeſtides; and that is Thales. Then comes Pittacus, and the reſt of them. There are ſeven, you ſee, in all.

MENIPPUS.

They are the only perſons, who appear cheerful, and unconcerned. But who is he all covered with aſhes? He has a ſkin as full of bliſters as a cake baked in the cinders.

ÆACUS.

That gentleman is Empedocles, who came hither half-roaſted from mount Ætna.

MENIPPUS.

Pray, my good Mr. Brazenfoot, what could induce you to throw yourſelf into the craters of Ætna?

EMPEDOCLES.

I was not quite right in my head, I believe, Menippus.

MENIPPUS.

I believe so too; but it was vanity, and pride, and folly, that made you so. The consequence of which has been, that not only yourself, who richly deserved it, but your innocent flippers too, are reduced to a cinder. Your ingenious device availed you nothing, except proving the death of you.—But where is Socrates all this while?

ÆACUS.

Socrates generally passes his time in trifling with Nestor and Palamede.

MENIPPUS.

If he is any where hereabouts, I should be very glad to have a sight of him.

ÆACUS.

Do you see that man with the bald head?

MENIPPUS.

I see nothing else but bald heads: a bald head, as far as I can perceive, is no distinction at all here.

ÆACUS.

ÆACUS.

I mean him with the flat nose.

MENIPPUS.

There again! they have all flat noses, I tell you.

SOCRATES.

Are you enquiring after me, Menippus?

MENIPPUS.

Yes, Socrates, indeed I am.

SOCRATES.

How go matters at Athens?

MENIPPUS.

Very many of the younger sort profess themselves philosophers. And truly, were you to judge of them by their habit and their gait, you might venture to pronounce them philosophers with a witness.

SOCRATES.

I have seen several of that sort.

MENIPPUS.

And you cannot be a stranger, I think, to the appearance, which Aristippus and Plato made, when they came hither. The former was all over perfume; and the latter came to you instructed in the various arts of flattery, which he had so successfully practised on the [g] kings of Sicily.

SOCRATES.

Pray, Sir, what do they say of me?

MENIPPUS.

In some respects they speak very well of you. Nay, all are ready to acknowledge you a very extraordinary man, who knew every thing; when, in good truth, as you yourself declared, you knew nothing.

SOCRATES.

How often I told them so! But truly they must needs think me in jest!

---

[g] If we may trust Cornelius Nepos, the flattery of Plato was somewhat differently directed from that of most other courtiers. Plato autem tantum apud Dionysium autoritate potuit, valuitque eloquentia ut persuaserit tyrannidis facere finem, libertatemque reddere Syracusanis.

Vita Dionis, p. 129. Keuchen's Edition.

MENIPPUS.

Who are these near you?

SOCRATES.

These, Menippus, are Charmides, and Phædrus, and the son of Clinias.

MENIPPUS.

I find you are no changeling, Socrates; you are as fond as ever of youth and beauty.

SOCRATES.

What would you have me do? But come, stay here with us; will you?

MENIPPUS.

No; I am going to be near Crœsus and Sardanapalus, where, I presume, I shall not be disappointed of some entertainment in attending to their lamentations.

ÆACUS.

And I must go and look after my dead, that none of them give me the flip. Another time you shall see more.

MENIPPUS.

I beg I may not any longer detain you: what I have already seen is quite sufficient.

MENIPPUS AND TANTALUS.

MENIPPUS.

WHAT is the meaning of this, Tantalus? Why do you stand in this manner weeping and wailing over the lake?

TANTALUS.

I weep, Menippus, because I am ready to die with thirst.

MENIPPUS.

What, are you so very lazy, that you will not so much as bend your neck, or hold out your hand, to supply yourself with a little drink?

TANTALUS.

To stoop down is to no manner of purpose, for the water perceives my approach, and avoids me. And, if I take up a little in the hollow of my hand, I can no sooner wet my lips, than it slips through my fingers in a most unaccountable manner, leaving my hand perfectly dry.

MENIPPUS.

What you relate, Tantalus, is very strange indeed. Though, to be plain with you, I cannot see any occasion you can have for drink. Your body, that part of you which was subject to hunger and thirst, lies buried in Lydia. And your soul, which is all you possess at present, can hardly be supposed to want either meat or drink.

TANTALUS.

That is the mischief of it. What you observe is quite right. But, though I have no body, I am sentenced to endure the sensations of hunger and thirst, just in the same manner as if I had one.

MENIPPUS.

Since you tell us, that such is your punishment, we are bound to believe what you say. But, admitting all you assert, what is there so very terrible in it? You need not be afraid here of dying for want of drink. For I do not see,

that

that there is any other hell after this, or any other death to conduct you to it.

TANTALUS.

Very true. But this is what my punishment partly confists in, to long for what I do not want.

MENIPPUS.

You muft be out of your fenfes, Tantalus: the only drink that you really ftand in need of is a good large draught of Hellebore. Your diforder is the very reverfe of that which is occafioned by the bite of a mad dog; for it is not water, but the want of water, which you dread!

TANTALUS.

So that I could but drink, I fhould be contented to drink even Hellebore!

MENIPPUS.

Make yourfelf eafy, Tantalus; it cannot be that either you, or any other of the dead, fhould tafte one drop of liquor. Indeed your companions do not feel the want of it, not being punifhed in the fame manner.

DIOGENES AND HERCULES.

DIOGENES.

IS not this Hercules? By Hercules it is! The bow, the club, the lion's skin, the size, put it out of all doubt. It is Hercules himself, and nobody else. The son of Jupiter dead? How is it with you [b], Callinicus, are you really dead or no? I took you for a god when I was on earth, and sacrificed to you accordingly.

HERCULES.

You did very right, and no more than your duty. Hercules himself resides with the gods in heaven, possessing fair-footed Hebe. And I am his [i] image here.

DIO.

---

[b] Καλλινικος, graced with victory, an epithet given to Hercules in a hymn of Archilochus, sung at the Olympick games. Καλλινικ' αναξ Ἡρακλης.

[i] " Now I the strength of Hercules behold,
" A tow'ring spectre of gigantick mould,
" A * shadowy form! for high in heav'n's abodes
" Himself resides, a god among the gods;
" There in the bright assemblies of the skies
" He nectar quaffs, and Hebe crowns his joys."

* The image, or αδωλον, descends into the regions of the departed; and the soul, or the divine part of man, is received into heaven: thus the

body

DIOGENES.

What do you say? An image of a god? Is it poſſible? Can the ſame perſon at the ſame time be half a god and half a mortal?

HERCULES.

Nothing more certain. Hercules did not die, it was only I his image.

DIOGENES.

O your ſervant! Now I begin to underſtand you: Hercules gave you up to Pluto as his ſubſtitute; you died in his room.

HERCULES.

Yes.

body of Hercules was conſumed in the flames, his image is in hell, and his ſoul in heaven. There is a beautiful moral couched in the fable of his being married to Hebe, or youth, after death; to imply, that a perpetual youth, or a reputation which never grows old, is the reward of thoſe heroes, who like Hercules employ their courage for the good of human kind." Pope's Odyſſey, XL 741, &c.

An old epigram makes four parts of a man:

"Bis duo ſunt homines, manes, caro, ſpiritus, umbra;
"Quattuor has partes tot loca ſuſcipiunt.
"Terra tegit carnem; tumulum circumvolat umbra;
"Orcus habet manes; ſpiritus aſtra petit."

DIOGENES.

How happened it, that Æacus, who keeps so good a look-out, did not discover the trick? I thought he could not have been induced to take any Hercules but the true one.

HERCULES.

Only consider, Sir, I was the very picture of him.

DIOGENES.

There I believe you. The picture was so very like, that it was the very original. I believe you mistake your story: you are Hercules, and it is your image that is married to Hebe.

HERCULES.

You are an impertinent saucy fellow, I can say that. And, if you do not think fit immediately to desist from your ill-manners, you shall very soon be made sensible whose image I am.

DIOGENES.

I know very well, that you are but a [*k*] word and a blow. Yet, as I am dead, I see no great

---

[*k*] A word and a blow. The original is, *your bow is naked and ready*, not in the case, which was a thing usual amongst the antients. See Iob. id. X. Sub.

occasion to be afraid of you. But, in the name of your own Hercules, I conjure you to tell me, were you his image living, an adjunct of him then; or, rather, were you one during life? and, being parted by death, he took his flight to the gods above; while you, as one might expect of an image, made your way down hither.

HERCULES.

Though I might very fairly be excused making any reply to such an ironical asker of questions, yet I will tell you so much as this; whatever there was of Amphitryon in the composition of Hercules, I am all that, and that is dead; but what there was of Jupiter in him lives in heaven with the gods.

DIOGENES.

I understand you now very well. You mean to say, that Alcmena brought forth two Herculeses at the same time, the one by Amphitryon, the other by Jupiter. This was kept a secret. The world was not made acquainted with Alcmena's bearing twins.

HERCULES.

Twins! Do not miſtake yourſelf. I alone am all the twins ſhe bore.

DIOGENES.

Two in one! This is not quite ſo eaſy of digeſtion: unleſs I ſuppoſe the god and man compounded like the centaur.

HERCULES.

Do not you allow that all men whatever are made up of two parts, ſoul and body? What then ſhould hinder the ſoul, which proceeded from Jupiter, from being in heaven; whilſt I, the part produced by man, am here amongſt the dead?

DIOGENES.

My good ſon of Amphitryon, you might talk in this manner, if you had a body; but you are nothing more than an incorporeal image. But perhaps you may be diſpoſed to ſplit Hercules into three.

HERCULES.

How, into three?

DIOGENES.

In this manner. One, you tell us, is in heaven; you, the image, are here with us; and the body lies on mount Oeta, a lump of dust. There are three parts of him, you must allow, by this plain way of reckoning. So it rests with you still to find out a father for the body.

HERCULES.

You are some sly impudent fellow or other. Pray what is your name?

DIOGENES.

I am the image of Diogenes of Sinope. I do not pretend to [1] associate with gods; but I keep the very best company here, where I divert myself with laughing at the insipid conceits of Homer.

[1] Hercules is represented by Homer, Od. XI. 600, as passing his time very jovially with Hebe and the gods.

ACHILLES.

ACHILLES AND ANTILOCHUS.

ANTILOCHUS.

WHAT [m] was it, Achilles, I heard you say to Ulysses the other day concerning death? What a speech! how mean and pitiful! how unworthy the disciple of Chiron and Phœnix! You openly declared, that you had rather let yourself out for hire, and become the poor slave of some rustick who is himself half-starved, than remain here on condition of being monarch of all the dead. Such a thought might have been suitable enough to a poor dastardly Trojan, pitifully preferring his life to every other consideration. But that the son of Peleus, the most daring of heroes, should harbour such groveling sentiments, is in truth not only a great shame, but a most glaring contradiction to every action of his life! who, when he might have reigned secure many years

---

[m] Rather I choose laboriously to bear
A weight of woes, and breathe the vital air,
A slave to some poor hind, that toils for bread,
Than reign the scepter'd monarch of the dead.
     Pope's Hom. Od. XI. 600.

See also the note.

at Phthiotis, found no difficulty in preferring death and fame to an inglorious life.

ACHILLES.

At that time, O son of Nestor, I was not acquainted with what passes here: otherwise you may depend upon it, that nothing but entire ignorance could have induced me to make so ridiculous a choice. But I am now no longer a stranger to the real value of that contemptible glory, which fills so many mouths on earth with its praises. No distinction whatever reaches this state. All are exactly alike. Here, Antilochus, neither beauty nor strength is of the least avail. We are all immersed in the same obscurity, without any manner of difference. I, for instance, am neither feared by the Trojans, nor regarded by the Greeks. Every one is here on the same footing; and, when once a man is dead, it makes not the least difference, whether he had courage, or whether he had none. These considerations so disconcert and vex me, that I cannot avoid wishing for life on any terms.

ANTILOCHUS.

But why should you want to revolt from the law of nature, which ordains all men to die without diftinction? As you are included in that univerfal edict, you fhould reft contented, without fretting at that which muft inevitably come to pafs. Befides, do not you fee how many of your friends are here affembled on all fides of you? And Ulyffes too will moft certainly be here by and by. If this be fuffering, you will fuffer in good company; and that is fome comfort. Only look round you! There is Hercules, and there is Meleager, and there are many other illuftrious perfonages, who, I am confident, would fcorn to think of returning to life on fuch beggarly terms as you propofe!

ACHILLES.

I own you talk like a friend. But I know not how it is, the remembrance of life grievoufly afflicts me; as, indeed, I fhrewdly fufpect, it does all of you. If you do not vouchfafe to confefs it, your fuffering in filence only makes the matter fo much the worfe.

ANTILOCHUS.

You are very much mistaken: our behaviour is much more becoming persons situated as we are. We see it is to no manner of purpose to complain of our fate, and have therefore resolved to bear it with patience, without exposing ourselves to be laughed at, as you do, by a repetition of ridiculous wishes.

ALEXANDER AND PHILIP.

PHILIP.

I SUPPOSE now, Alexander, you will hardly deny your being my son. For you would not have died, you know, if you had been the son of Jupiter Ammon.

ALEXANDER.

I never entertained any doubt of my being the son of Philip, and the grandson of Amyntas; but I closed in with what was delivered by the Oracle, as supposing it would be useful to me in my affairs.

PHILIP.

PHILIP.

What, did you think it so good a thing to be made a fool of by soothsayers?

ALEXANDER.

No, I do not say that. But I can assure you, Sir, the Barbarians were so struck with the idea, that nobody dared to think of opposing me. It was in vain to contend with a god, and therefore I had an easy victory.

PHILIP.

An easy victory over whom? I should be glad to know what people you ever subdued, that deserved to be called soldiers? It is true, you ventured to engage with a few cowardly fellows, armed with paltry bows and willow shields, equally insignificant with themselves. But that was not conquering the Greeks. To have vanquished the Bœotians, or the Phocensians, or Athenians, the heavy-armed Arcadians, the Thessalian horse, the javelin-darting Elæans, the shield-bearing Mantineans; to have subdued the Thracians, or Illyrians, or Pæonians, would have been something to talk of. Did you never hear, that under the command of Clearchus, before your time, an army of no more than ten thousand men vanquished the Medes, the Persians, and Chaldæans? Those highly polished gentlemen, with so much gold and finery, were too delicate to hazard their persons in an engagement; and, before the impression of one arrow, prudently betook themselves to flight.

ALEXANDER.

But then the Scythians, father, and the elephants of India—what do you say to them? That, I believe, was no very contemptible business. These victories were neither obtained by sowing sedition, nor buying treachery. I never forswore myself, never promised what I did not mean to perform, never forfeited my honour for the sake of conquest. Of the Greeks, [a] a great part were added to my empire without bloodshed. And you have heard, perhaps, how I punished the Thebans.

PHILIP.

Yes, I have. Clitus told me, whom you killed at a feast, Clitus who was run through

[a] 'Ελληνες, the inhabitants of that division of the Grecian territories called Hellas. Greece, properly so called, consisted of Achaia, Peloponnesus, and the islands.

the body for presuming to extol my actions above yours. Laying aside the Macedonian [*] chlamys, you assumed the Persian [*] candys, you put on the tiara. You even ventured to think yourself an object of the adoration of your free countrymen. What was most ridiculous in your conduct, you constantly mimicked the customs of those which you had conquered. Not to mention other enormities, your practice was to shut up men of learning in the dens of lions. Your marriages too were equally indefensible, as was your unwarrantable fondness for Hephæstion. There was one circumstance in your behaviour, which, I must own, I could not but commend you for: you made no unbecoming offers to the beautiful wife of Darius. In that, and in your care of his mother and daughters, you acted as became a king.

ALEXANDER.

And have you nothing, Sir, to say in praise of me for my readiness in facing danger? I was the very first man, you may remember, who scaled the walls of Oxydracæ, where I was welcomed with numberless wounds.

[*] Worn by the soldiers of Macedonia and Persia.

PHILIP.

I do not admire your conduct there. Not that I see any impropriety in a king's expoſing himſelf to be wounded, and being the firſt to ruſh into danger, on certain occaſions. But this was by no means prudent in you: yours was a particular caſe. Only ſuppoſe the general, who has had the good fortune of being eſteemed a god, to be grievouſly wounded, and to be ſeen carried off from the battle, flowing with blood, on the back of a porter, would not he and his lamentations be ſufficient to excite the laughter of all beholders? The wizard Ammon, the lying ſoothſayer, the flattering fortune-tellers, would be words of courſe in every body's mouth. The ſon of Jupiter fainting away, and requiring the ſkill of the ſurgeon, could never be a fight for a grave man to ſee. Pray, Sir, now you are dead, do not you obſerve numbers ſcoffing and jeering at your ſilly pretences? Think of the divine carcaſe of a ſwollen god laid out at length, and ſtinking like mere mortality! As to the eaſe, with which you ſay you obtained your victories, that very circumſtance robbed you of half your

glory,

glory. For whatever might otherwise have appeared important became nothing at all, when confidered as the act of a god.

ALEXANDER.

Other people do not talk of my exploits as you do. I am ranked with Hercules, and Bacchus—nay, I alone furmounted [p] Aornus, which neither of them could do.

PHILIP.

Are you not yet afhamed of giving yourfelf thefe airs? But it is the fon of Ammon, no doubt, who compares himfelf to Bacchus and Hercules. Fie for fhame! fon Alexander, have done with your arrogance! Now you are dead, cannot you learn a little modefty, and honeftly own yourfelf to be what you really are?

[p] A rock in India, which Alexander eafily poffeffed himfelf of, though reported by hiftorians as inacceffible, even to the birds of the air.

DIOGENES AND ALEXANDER.

DIOGENES.

WHAT means this, Alexander? What, are you dead too, like all the reſt of us?

ALEXANDER.

You ſee I am. Is it any wonder, that a man ſhould die?

DIOGENES.

No, to be ſure. So then Jupiter Ammon told a fib, when he ſaid you were his ſon! You were the ſon of Philip all the while!

ALEXANDER.

The ſon of Philip, moſt aſſuredly. I ſhould not have died, you know, if I had been the ſon of Jupiter.

DIOGENES.

What idle reports were ſpread concerning Olympias! that your mother had been ſeen in bed with a monſtrous ſerpent! that you were the conſequence of that extraordinary commerce! Mean while poor Philip, who believed himſelf

himself to be your father, was miserably imposed upon!

ALEXANDER.

I have heard such stories as well as you. But I now perceive very plainly, that my mother and the prophets of Ammon were all liars alike, who never uttered a word that was true.

DIOGENES.

However, Sir, you must allow, that their lying was of no inconsiderable service to you. What numbers really believed you to be a god, and were for that reason ready to drop down dead with the fear of you! But pray, Alexander, who succeeds you in your vast dominions?

ALEXANDER.

I do not know, Diogenes. I had no opportunity of determining that point. All I could do was to give my ring to Perdiccas, as I was dying. Pray, Sir, what do you find to laugh at?

DIOGENES.

I was only thinking of your being so be-praised by the Greeks, when you came first to your empire, that you alone were deemed fit

for

for power, and nobody else would do for their leader against the barbarians. Some of them were ready to enroll you with the twelve divinities. They built temples to your honour, and offered sacrifices to the son of the serpent! —But I want to know where the Macedonians have buried you.

ALEXANDER.

At present I remain at Babylon, where I have been these [q] three days. But I am promised by Ptolemy, my armour-bearer, that, as soon as ever he can obtain a little rest from the present disturbances, he will carry me into Ægypt, and bury me there, where I am to be an Ægyptian god.

DIOGENES.

Really, Alexander, this is enough to make any body laugh, to see you still playing the fool even here! What, I suppose, you expect to be an Anubis or Osiris! I beg of you, most divine Sir, not to deceive yourself so egregiously. When you have once passed over the lake, and have got on this side of yonder en-

[q] Alexander lay unburied at Babylon thirty days, while his friends were disputing about the succession. Ælian. v. 4. lib. 64.

trance,

trance, it is an absolute impossibility to get back again: Æacus is not so negligent of his duty, and Cerberus is always on his guard. I should be glad to know, Alexander, how you bear the remembrance of your past happiness. Your [r] life-guards, your [r] shield-bearers, your [r] nobles, your accumulating [r] gold, your [r] adoring nations, your [r] Babylon, your [r] Bactra, your [r] wild beasts, [r] your honour, [r] your glory, your [r] riding in state, your [r] head bound with a white fillet, your [r] purple so finely buttoned—Does not all this vex you, when you think of it? But you are not so silly as to weep. No doubt the wise Aristotle instructed you better than that you should be grieved at the inconstancy of fortune.

ALEXANDER.

The wise Aristotle, as you call him, was the very worst of sycophants. You will give me leave to be well acquainted with him. I have not forgot the requests that he made, and the messages which he sent. I had a passionate love

[r] This enumeration of the several particulars of regal felicity is recommended to the consideration of those whom it may concern.

of learning, and he turned it to a bad use. I lived in a continual course of flattery. One while he praised me for my beauty (as if forsooth that were such a mighty matter); another while he admired my exploits. Then he could not help extolling me for my riches. Money, you must know, he considered as something substantial, which a man need not be ashamed to receive. But you cannot imagine, Diogenes, how very artful, how very cunning he is. One great advantage, which I have derived from his instructions, is to mourn and lament immoderately for the loss of those fine things you have mentioned, as if I had been deprived of the greatest good.

DIOGENES.

Do not you know what is proper to be done on this occasion? Though Hellebore does not grow here, I can prescribe a remedy for your grief. You have nothing more to do than to swallow a large draught of Lethe, repeating it again and again, till you become perfectly indifferent about the chief good of Aristotle. But behold! I see Clitus, and Callisthenes, and many others, hurrying this way. They all retain such a grateful sense of your favours, that,

I be-

I believe, they will seize the first opportunity of tearing you to pieces! Take my advice; step out of their way, and do not forget what I said concerning the Lethe.

ALEXANDER, ANNIBAL, MINOS, AND SCIPIO.

ALEXANDER.

YOU do not think of being admitted to trial [s] sooner than your betters, Mr. Libyan?

ANNIBAL.

No. But I think of being tried before you.

[s] Scipio, having an interview with Annibal at Ephesus, after other conversation, asked him, who, in his opinion, was the greatest general that ever appeared in the world. Annibal answered, Alexander. And whom do you consider, said Scipio, as next to him? Pyrrhus, replied Annibal. And who is the next to him? said Scipio? Myself, said Annibal, without all manner of doubt. Upon this Scipio smiled, and asked him, What he would have thought of himself, if he had conquered him. I should have thought myself, replied Annibal, greater than Pyrrhus, and greater than Alexander, and the greatest of all great commanders. Livy, vi. 35.

ALEX-

ALEXANDER.

If you entertain any doubt who ought to have the preference, let Minos determine between us.

MINOS.

Before I determine any thing, let me know who you are.

ALEXANDER.

This gentleman is Annibal, the Carthaginian; and I am Alexander, the son of Philip.

MINOS.

Both very respectable names! Pray, what do you find to quarrel about [t] here?

ALEXANDER.

Precedency. He pretends truly to be a greater general than Alexander! when all the world knows, that I not only far excelled him, but, I believe I may venture to say, every body else that lived before me.

[t] The reader will pardon the insertion of the little word "here," which is not in the original.

MINOS.

MINOS.

Let me know your respective pretensions,
And first I would hear what the Libyan has to
say.

ANNIBAL.

I have this advantage to begin with, Minos,
that I understand [u] Greek as well as he does.
And, in my opinion, they deserve the greatest
praise, who derive the fewest claims from the
merit of others; who, being themselves originally nothing at all, do, notwithstanding all obstructions, make their way to greatness, and
arrive at power by their own proper desert. At
first, serving under my [x] brother, and advancing with a handful of men into Spain, I
so distinguished myself, as to be thought equal
to the highest command. I reduced the Celtiberians, and conquered the western Galatians.
Traversing vast mountains, I over-ran the whole
country about the Po. I razed many cities. I
subdued the whole of the plains of Italy, and

[u] According to the testimony of Cornelius Nepos and
others, Annibal understood Greek and Latin too, particularly
the former, having written several books in that language.

[x] Asdrubal, his sister's husband.

advanced

advanced even to the suburbs of the principal
city. I slew such a number of men in one day,
that I measured their rings in [*y*] bushels, and
made bridges over the rivers with their dead
bodies. And all this I did without being re-
puted the son of Jupiter Ammon, without pretending to be a god, without so much as telling my mother's dreams. When engaged with
the most experienced generals, who commanded
armies of the most hardy veterans, I made no
scruple of honestly owning myself to be a man.
It was not with such as the Medes and Armenians that I contended, men who fly though
there are none to pursue, and who fail not instantly to yield the victory to any one who has
courage enough only to claim it. Alexander,
it must be confessed, very much increased and
extended the limits of his father's empire, for
which he may thank his good-fortune; and,
being flushed with conquest, after vanquishing

[*y*] This was after the famous victory obtained over the
Romans at Cannæ. The accounts concerning the quantity
of rings sent to Carthage do not entirely agree; some authors,
as Livy for example, seem to think one bushel a very handsome allowance. Livy 25. Besides, the Roman modius, which
we translate bushel, according to Arbuthnot, is in English
measure little more than a peck.

the

the wretched Darius at Iſſus and Arbeli, nothing would ſerve him but divine worſhip. The god was reſolved to be a god indeed. Notwithſtanding he preſently degenerated from Philip who begat him, and aſſumed the cuſtoms and manners of the effeminate Medes. He polluted his banquets with the blood of his friends, whom he diſdained not to ſeize and put to death. I too was inveſted by my country with the ſupreme command, and when that country thought fit to recall me, at the very time that a great fleet of the enemy had ſailed to invade Libya, I made no heſitation, but immediately obeyed. I directly reſigned all my power, and became as much as ever a private man. Even when judgment was given againſt me, I patiently ſubmitted. In this manner I conducted myſelf and the affairs of my country, being a barbarian, uninſtructed in the learning of the elegant Greeks, and not, like Alexander, able to repeat all Homer by heart. I had not the advantage of having had the precepts of Ariſtotle to profit by, but owed every thing to my own genius. Theſe, Sir, are my reaſons for preſuming to think myſelf ſuperior to Alexander. If indeed he values himſelf on having his head bound up with a fine diadem, such a pretension, for aught I know, may pass with the Macedonians; but, I fancy, so silly a conceit should hardly exalt his merit above that of a spirited and discerning general, who derived much less of his success from the impulse of fortune, than the prudence of his counsels, and the native powers of his own mind.

MINOS.

It is now your turn to speak, Alexander. Upon my word he has acquitted himself in a much better manner than could have been expected from one of his country.

ALEXANDER.

It is quite unnecessary surely, Minos, for Alexander to make any reply to so audacious a claim. Let it suffice, that Fame has recorded me as a great king, and him as a great [y] thief. I pray, Sir, consider the difference! I succeeded to the empire very young, and found my affairs

[y] Alexander himself, and many others as good, have been called very opprobrious names by saucy wits. Demosthenes bestows on Philip, the father of Alexander, the very same appellation, which Alexander in this dialogue gives to Annibal, λυτης, a free-booter, or publick robber. Philipp. 4.

In a very bad situation. I immediately put an end to the disorders that prevailed in the state. I revenged myself on the murderers of my father, and threw all Greece into a consternation by the destruction of the Thebans. Being appointed to the command of their armies, I thought it a pitiful ambition to be master of the Macedonians alone, and to rest contented with the care of cherishing merely what my father had left me. I compassed in my imagination the circuit of the earth, and was persuaded, that, unless I could conquer the whole of it, I should be nobody at all. At the head therefore of my little army I advanced into Asia. I came off victorious in a great battle at the river Granicus. After making myself master of Lydia, Ionia, and Phrygia, and subduing whatever else lay in my way, I arrived at Issus, where Darius with a prodigious army waited my coming. After this, Minos, it is impossible that you can have forgot how many dead I dispatched to you in a single day. Charon declares, that his boat was so far from being capable of containing them, that very great numbers were obliged to cross the river on rafts, which they found themselves under a necessity of providing on that occasion. Whilst engaged in these exploits, I was so little in fear of being wounded, that I was always the first to rush into danger. Not to trouble you with the particulars of what passed at Tyre and Arbeli, I shall just mention my advancing to the Indies, where I bounded my empire with the ocean. I made their elephants my prisoners. I subdued Porus. Passing the Tanais, I beat the hardy Scythians in a great battle of cavalry. I employed myself in doing good to my friends, and taking vengeance on my enemies. And, if men took me for a god, they may very well be excused: it was natural enough to believe any thing of a person, whose actions were such as mine. The last thing I shall mention is, that I continued a great king to the end of my life. Whereas Annibal died in exile at the court of Prusias the Bithynian, as it was fit he should: a fellow so cruel deserved no better fate. It is needless to observe by what means he overcame the Italians; not by bravery, but superior villainy, perfidy, and deceit. Not one instance can be produced of his acting honourably, openly, and fairly. But, since he has thought fit to reproach me for my luxury, I fancy the

gentle-

gentleman muſt have forgot his own pretty doings at Capua; where, inſtead of improving his advantages, and ſeizing the favourable occaſions of war, he waſted his time with harlots, in a continued round of voluptuous idleneſs. For my part, if I had not diſtinguiſhed myſelf in the eaſtern world, I ſhould not have claimed much from my victories in the weſt. Though I made myſelf maſter of Italy without bloodſhed, though I ſubdued Libya, and the whole country as far as Gades, I looked upon all that as nothing. For what was it to conquer thoſe who trembled at my very name, and who, as ſoon as they could know my mind, were ready to acknowledge me their lord? I have done, Minos. From the little I have ſaid you will have no difficulty in deciding the matter between us.

SCIPIO.

Before you give judgment, Minos, I expect to be heard.

MINOS.

Pray, my good friend, what have you to ſay? Who are you? Whence come you?

SCIPIO.

SCIPIO.

I am Scipio, the Italian. I am the general who beat the Carthaginians in many pitched battles, and destroyed their city.

MINOS.

Well, and what then?

SCIPIO.

I do not mean, Sir, to compare myself with Alexander; but surely my actions may be allowed to be superior to those of Annibal, whom I conquered, whom I drove to a disgraceful flight. I wonder he is not ashamed to put himself in competition with Alexander; which is a great deal more than I who beat him dare presume to do!

MINOS.

I must confess, Scipio, that what you say carries a great deal of weight with it. Let Alexander stand first on the list to be tried, and Scipio next. And let Annibal, if he think fit, be the third. Annibal is not a character to be despised.

CRATES

CRATES AND DIOGENES.

CRATES.

PRAY, Diogenes, did you know the rich Mærichus? I mean the very wealthy Corinthian with such a quantity of shipping, the rich cousin of rich Aristeas. Aristeas was well enough disposed to his relation, to use with great propriety the words of Homer:

[z] "Do you fling me, my friend, or I will you."

DIOGENES.

What was the occasion of such compliments passing between them?

---

[z] Hom. Il. 23. v. 724. The words of Ajax wrestling with Ulysses, thus translated:

"Or let me lift thee, chief, or lift thou me."

which line of Pope's is not much more poetical than one of his master Dryden, in his translation of the interview between Hector and Andromache. Hom. Il. 6.

"He found her not at home, for she was gone."

"He found her not at home," says the great Dryden—and then adds this incomparable reason,—"for she was gone." With such symptoms of human frailty in the works of great authors, we little scribblers are marvellously apt to console ourselves!

CRATES.

Money, Sir, money. They were of the same age, and each had avowedly made his will in favour of the other; so that it was the interest of each, you see, to outlive the other, as it was the endeavour of each to out-flatter the other. The soothsayers, from the stars, or from dreams, deducing their skill (so were wont the sons of Chaldæa, and so Apollo himself), were by no means uniform in their judgment, deciding sometimes in favour of Aristeas, sometimes of Mœrichus. Now this end of the balance prevailed, and now [a] that.

DIOGENES.

But how did the affair end? I should be glad to hear.

CRATES.

They both died on the very same day; and their estates came to Eunomius and Thrasycles; who, though the next of kin, had never once had the least fore-boding of their own good fortune. The two friends, Aristeas and Mœri-

---

[a] Ζευς γαρ τοι το ταλαντον, οτε ρεπει αλλοτε αλλῃ,
Αλλοτε μεν πλουτειν, αλλοτε δ᾽ ουδεν εχειν.
Theognides, 157. B.

chus,

chus, having got about half way on a voyage from Sicyon to Cirrha, met with contrary winds, and were shipwrecked.

DIOGENES.

I am glad of it with all my heart. When you and I were in the world above, I think, we entertained no such sentiments the one towards the other. I never wished for the death of Antisthenes, that I might inherit his staff (though it was a good strong one, I remember, made of a wild olive); nor do I imagine, that you wished to survive me, or entertained any hopes of being heir to my estate, my tub, and my wallet, the latter of which held about [b] three pints of lupines.

CRATES.

We had no need of such things: you inherited of Autisthenes all that you wanted; and I succeeded you in a possession of more importance than the Persian empire.

[b] Two chænices. A chænix was a measure containing the quantity of victuals allowed by the Greeks to a slave for one day.

DIO-

DIOGENES.

What do you mean?

CRATES.

I mean wisdom, self-satisfaction, truth, liberty of sentiment, freedom of speech.

DIOGENES.

Yes, I well remember the estate which Antisthenes bequeathed me; it afterwards descended to you, I believe I may say, somewhat improved.

CRATES.

Yet nobody followed or flattered us with a view of inheriting our possessions; mean while money engaged universal attention.

DIOGENES.

They had no faculties for the reception of such treasures as ours. Their luxurious souls were as incontinent as a rotten purse. Not having a sound bottom, they are unable to retain wisdom, truth, and liberty; which would not fail to run through their minds as fast as they should be poured in. So that their condition resembles that of the daughters of Danaus, whose

whose task was to fill sieves with water. With regard to gold, it does not so readily escape them: to gold they cling with every [*c*] power they have,

CRATES.

However we have the better of them, because we can bring our riches with us even hither; while the utmost which they can secure is one sorry obolus, and that not for themselves, but the ferryman.

CHARON, MERCURY, and several of the Dead.

CHARON.

ONLY consider our situation. You see, gentlemen, the boat is not only very small, but very leaky, being somewhat the worse for wear; so that the least inclination to either side would infallibly overset us. And yet you come crowding in in such numbers, and every one of you so loaded, that, if you persist in carrying all this luggage, I am confident you will find

[*c*] ὀδοῦσι καὶ ὄνυξι. Tooth and nail.

reason to repent it, at least such of you as cannot swim.

THE DEAD.

What must we do to get safe over?

CHARON.

I will tell you what you must do. You must strip off those superfluities, leave them on the sand, and go aboard naked. Even then the boat will hardly contain you. Do you take good care, Mercury, that no one be taken in, who has not made himself as light as possible, quitting every thing which he intended to take with him. Stand by the ladder, and take an exact account of them. Oblige them to strip themselves stark naked; do you hear? Otherwise do not admit them.

MERCURY.

I hear what you say; I will take care. Who is this that comes first?

MENIPPUS.

Menippus. Here is my wallet, Mercury, and my staff; let them be tossed into the lake together. I was right not to bring my cloak.

MERCURY.

Welcome, my dear Menippus, thou best of men! Take the first seat, the high seat next to the waterman. There you may have the best opportunity of making observations on your companions. What fine fellow is this?

CHARMOLEUS.

I am the lovely Charmoleus of Megara; a kiss of me was rated at a [*d*] couple of talents.

MERCURY.

You must off with all your charms: this is no place for kissing. Away with that fine long hair, those glowing blushes, that delicate skin. Very well; you will do now. Get aboard.— But who are you, who look so gruff, with your purple, and your diadem?

LAMPICHUS.

I am Lampichus, the tyrant of the Geloi.

MERCURY.

But pray, Lampichus the tyrant of the Geloi, why so loaded?

[*d*] Three hundred eighty-seven pounds, ten shillings. Somewhat of the dearest.

LAMPICHUS.

I hope, Mercury, you did not expect a king to come naked?

MERCURY.

A king indeed! you are neither more nor less than a dead man, and as such I consider you. Away, Sir, with your fooleries!

LAMPICHUS.

My riches are gone already, you see.

MERCURY.

And your pride, and your arrogance, must be laid aside; unless you mean to overload the boat.

LAMPICHUS.

Well, but you will allow me to retain my diadem and my royal robe?

MERCURY.

Indeed, Sir, no such thing. Strip! strip!

LAMPICHUS.

What is to be done now? I have nothing left now that you can object to.

MERCURY.

Only a few trifling particulars, such as your cruelty, your folly, your insolence, your passion, and so forth.

LAMPICHUS.

At last, I hope I am light enough for you.

MERCURY.

Go aboard then.— What broad-shouldered, brawny fellow is this that comes next?

DAMASIAS.

Damasias, the wrestler.

MERCURY.

O, I remember you; I have seen you several times in the palæstra.

DAMASIAS.

Yes, Mercury; and you will not scruple taking me, for I am naked enough.

MERCURY.

I beg your pardon, Sir; I cannot think a man naked, whose bones are so well covered. In the state you are in, you would overturn the vessel with one foot. You must reduce your

fat

fat fides, caſt off your garlands, and part with your atchievements.

DAMASIAS.

Now you will allow me to be really naked, and in no more danger of ſinking the boat than another man.

MERCURY.

Get aboard then. You will find the advantage of being light.—You, Crato, muſt leave your riches, your delicacy, your luxury, your [*] poſthumous finery, the honours of your anceſtors. You are to forget all former claims of family, or dignity, even though you may have been publickly honoured as the benefactor of your country; the legend of the ſtatue, or the magnificence of the tomb, you are not to regard. Never mention them. The remembrance would only oppreſs you.

CRATO.

If I muſt part with them, I muſt. What can I do?

MERCURY.

Wonderful! a man in armour! What can this mean? For what, Sir, do you bear this trophy?

---

[*] πλαςια, the cloathing appropriated to dead bodies.

SOLDIER.

SOLDIER.

Because I have conquered. Because, Mercury, I have been honoured by my country. Because I have been distinguished above others.

MERCURY.

You had better leave your trophy behind you to be erected on earth: it would be preposterous in the world you are going to, where there is continual peace, and no use of arms.—But this venerable figure, perking up his eyes, and curling his brows, with such depth of cogitation and beard, who can he be?

MENIPPUS.

Some philosopher, you may be sure. Or, rather call him a Mountebank, a dealer in legerdemain. Do but strip him, and you will find many laughable articles concealed under his garment.

MERCURY.

You, Sir, first lay aside your habit, and then every thing else in order. O, Jupiter! what a collection! what arrogance, what ignorance, what wrangling, what vanity, what intricate questions, what thorny reasonings, what perplexed conceits, what labour in vain, what trifling, what foolery, what a noise about nothing, does this man carrry about him! Upon my word, Sir, before you go any further, you must dispose of your gold too. You must resolve to bid adieu to your good living. And it is now time to abandon your impudence, your pettishness, your luxury, your delicacy. Do not be so weak as to imagine you can conceal these, or any thing else from me. You must also part with your lying, and your pride, and give up that very favourable opinion which you entertain of your own superior merit. With all this baggage, Sir, a vessel with fifty oars would not hold you!

PHILOSOPHER.

You command, and I must obey.

MENIPPUS.

Pray, Mercury, would there be any impropriety in his laying aside that rough heavy beard

of

of his, which, I dare fay, does not weigh lefs than five minæ [ƒ]?

MERCURY.

You are in the right, Menippus. Off with it, Sir.

PHILOSOPHER.

But where is the barber?

MERCURY.

Menippus will undertake that office. The ship's ladder will ferve him for a block to lay it on, and he may chop it off with the carpenter's axe.

MENIPPUS.

Not with an axe, Mercury. I fhould prefer a faw: that would be better.

MURCURY.

The axe will do.

MENIPPUS.

Well, Sir, at prefent you look fomewhat more like a man, and ftink fomewhat lefs like a goat.—Suppofe I trim his eyebrows a little?

[ƒ] Four pounds, eight ounces, eighteen penny-weights, nine grains three-fevenths.

MERCURY.

By all means; I know not why he should hold them so high, or what he has to be so proud of.—What now, Sir? What, are you afraid of death? Come, come, get aboard.

MENIPPUS.

He has concealed one principal part of his load.

MERCURY.

What is that?

MENIPPUS.

His old friend adulation, which has been of such singular use to him.

PHILOSOPHER.

Since you come to that, Menippus, I beg you will strip too, and lay aside your impertinence. Leave off indulging your tongue in such unwarrantable liberties. Your daring unconcern, your railing, your derision, are not to be endured. Why should you be the only one to laugh?

MERCURY.

I say, let Menippus keep what he has. They are light commodities, easily portable, and very serviceable

serviceable in a voyage.—But you, Mr. Orator, you are to leave behind you your endless loquacity, your antitheses, the roundings of your periods, your barbarisms, your wordy lumber.

ORATOR.

Very well; I submit.

MERCURY.

You do right.—Come, let us get ready for sailing. Hoist up the ladder, and weigh anchor. Set your sail, and mind your steerage, Mr. Waterman. A good voyage to us! What do you find to weep for, ye fools! The Philosopher, who has been just shaved, seems inconsolable.

PHILOSOPHER.

I thought the soul of man immortal. It is that confideration, Mercury, which makes me weep.

MENIPPUS.

He lies, Mercury. His weeping is owing to a very different cause.

MERCURY.

What?

MENIPPUS.

He weeps because he shall no longer enjoy his delicious suppers, nor have an opportunity at night of stealing out, muffled up in his robe, to visit the brothels. He will no longer in a morning earn money by imposing on his young disciples his pretended wisdom. These are his grievances.

PHILOSOPHER.

And pray, Menippus, do you feel no concern at the thought of being no longer alive?

MENIPPUS.

I wonder you can ask the question. Did not I make all the [g] haste hither I could without call or compulsion?—But while we are thus talking, do not you hear a great noise, Mercury, which seems to be made by some people bawling above?

MERCURY.

I hear it very well; but it does not appear to proceed all from the same place. Some are running together to divert themselves, and laugh at the death of Lampichus. His wife

[g] Menippus hanged himself, if Diogenes Laertius is to be believed.

is pent up not very much to her satisfaction, within a circle of women. The boys are pelting his little children with great stones. In Sicyon several persons are extolling Diophantus, the orator, who has composed a funeral panegyrick on Craton. The mother of Damasias [b] leads the band of mourners for the loss of her son. But as for you, Menippus, nobody grieves for you, you alone may lie quiet.

MENIPPUS.

I beg your pardon. It will not be a great while before you will hear the dogs miserably howling over me, and the croaking ravens flapping their wings, in honour of my obsequies.

MERCURY.

You are a fine fellow, Menippus. But we are now at the end of our voyage. That path will take you directly to the place of trial. Meantime Charon and I must go back for more.

MENIPPPUS.

I wish you a good voyage with all my heart. Come, let us go forward. Pshaw! what signifies

[b] ἐξάρχει τῶ θρηνω σὺν γυναιξίν, begins the howl with her women.

this reluctance? you must all submit to your sentence, whether you like it or not. They talk of heavy punishments, such as wheels, and vultures, and huge stones; which, I can tell you for your comfort, you will find it impossible to evade; for every action of every one of you will be laid fully open.

SIMYLUS AND POLYSTRATUS.

SIMYLUS.

AND you are come amongst us at last, Polystratus! I believe you lived to near a hundred.

POLYSTRATUS.

I was ninety eight, Simylus, when I died.

SIMYLUS.

And how did you pass the last thirty years of your life? When I died, I think, you were about seventy.

POLYSTRATUS.

I do not know what you may think of the matter, but I can assure you I passed my time very agreeably.

SIMYLUS.

I cannot but marvel indeed, if a decrepit old fellow like you, and with never a child to comfort him, could find any thing delectable in life.

POLYSTRATUS.

Sir, I had every thing at my command. I was attended by a numerous retinue of the most beautiful of both sexes, all in the flower of their youth. I had the finest perfumes, and the most delicious wine; I had a table even exceeding that of a Sicilian.

SIMYLUS.

My wonder increases. For I well remember you used to be remarkably stingy and sparing of your expences.

POLYSTRATUS.

All these fine things, my good Sir, were the contributions of others, whose benefactions flowed upon me in a stream. My doors were crowded by day-break with multitudes waiting my levee. And the very moment of admittance, the most valuable presents of every kind came pouring in upon me from every corner of the earth.

SIMYLUS.

After I was dead then, I suppose, you became a king?

POLYSTRATUS.

No, I was no king; but, nevertheless, I had admirers without number.

SIMYLUS.

Admirers? you make a body laugh. Admirers! what did they admire? your four teeth and your five score years?

POLYSTRATUS.

You may be as witty as you please; what I say is true. I was, indeed, as you observe, somewhat old, rather bald, and rather blind, and my nose none of the cleanest; yet, notwithstanding all this, my lovers, who by the bye were the principal persons of the city, were most assiduous to shew their passion, and happy was he on whom I happened to cast a favourable glance.

SIMYLUS.

I know not what to make of all this, unless you are another [i] Phaon, Pray, have you, like him, given Venus a cast over the water? and did she, in return for your civil usage, grant you a wish? and was it in consequence of that, that you became young again and beautiful and lovely?

POLYSTRATUS.

I had no manner of occasion to make use of such high-flown pretences: every body was in love with me as I was, beauty without paint.

SIMYLUS.

You talk riddles.

POLYSTRATUS.

There is nothing strange nor mysterious in the matter. Love is continually lying in wait

---

[i] We are informed by Ælian, Var. Hist. XII, 18, that Phaon was a waterman, who, happening to have Venus for a passenger over the river, was so extremely civil, and took such uncommon care of her, that, at parting, she bestowed on him a box of cosmerick; by using which, he became so very handsome, that all the ladies of Mitylene fell in love with him, particularly Sappho, " quam scribere jussit amor."

for

for such amiable old fellows as have no heirs to their estates.

SIMYLUS.

Now, I fancy, I begin to understand you. Your beauty was the gift of the golden Venus.

POLYSTRATUS.

My lovers were almost ready to adore me; and, you may be sure, I made the most of it. I used to give myself airs, and order myself to be denied to them, and was as prudish as you please; meanwhile they were labouring with all their might to outdo one another in courtship and assiduity.

SIMYLUS.

But what did you resolve on at last with respect to your possessions?

POLYSTRATUS.

I used to give out, that I intended such an one for my heir, naming them all in their turns. Every one was thus induced to consider himself as the man that was meant, and of course became more and more complaisant. All this while I had no design in favour of any one of them, having bequeathed all my effects to quite a different person. To them, I can assure you,

I left

I left nothing more than a most miserable disappointment.

SIMYLUS.

And who then was appointed heir, by your last will and testament? the nearest akin, I suppose?

POLYSTRATUS.

No such thing, believe me. A handsome, young Phrygian, that I had just made a purchase of, was the man.

SIMYLUS.

Young, you say; pray what age might he be?

POLYSTRATUS.

About twenty.

SIMYLUS.

Sir, your most humble servant.

POLYSTRATUS.

Nay, I am sure he richly deserved my estate: the poor barbarian was much preferable to them. And so it appears, for the best of them is now not a little proud of being his friend. He, Sir, was my heir, and became from that moment of as good a family as any in the country.

country. Though his beard and his Greek are almost equally strangers to him, Codrus can at present no more surpass him in descent, than Nireus in Beauty, or Ulysses in wisdom.

SIMYLUS.

I care not what he is. He may be captain general of Greece if he will; so as he does but stand in the way between the flatterers and the fortune.

KNEMON AND DAMNIPPUS.

KNEMON.

THIS is verifying the proverb, catching a tartar!

DAMNIPPUS.

What is the matter, Knemon? you seem angry?

KNEMON.

Angry! I have reason enough to be angry. Blockhead as I was, how I have been outwitted! I have disposed of my estate quite contrary to my own intentions.

DAMNIPPUS.

How could that be?

KNEMON.

I will tell you. Hermolaus being extremely rich, and having no child, I thought him a proper object of my attention and assiduity. He readily accepted my services; and I as impatiently waited the event. I looked upon it as no bad scheme to shew my will, in which I had appointed him heir of all I had in the world; thinking he might be thus induced to return the compliment.

DAMNIPPPUS.

And did he not?

KNEMON.

How he settled his affairs in his last will and testament, I can give no account. I only know this, that I had the misfortune to die before him, being killed in a moment by the fall of a house. Upon which Hermolaus took immediate possession of all that was mine. He was as eager, Sir, as the pike, that greedily swallows both bait and hook———

DAMNIPPUS.

And fisherman too. You have been too cunning for yourself; that is all.

KNEMON.

Indeed I have, and I sorely repent it.

ZENOPHONTES AND CALLIDEMIDES.

ZENOPHANTES.

WHAT did you die of, Callidemides? As me, I was the parasite of Deinias, and was choaked by over-gorging myself. But you must remember it very well; you were by all the while.

CALLIDEMIDES.

I remember it very well. Mine was a more whimsical end. You could not but know old Ptæodorus.

ZENOPHANTES.

You mean the old man whom you used to be continually with. He was very rich, I remember, and had no children to inherit his fortune.

CALLIDEMIDES.

The very man. I was constantly employed in paying my court to him, thinking he would die at laſt, and leave me to enjoy the benefit of my labour. But he lived a moſt tedious while, even to be older than [k] Tithonus; which put me upon finding out what I thought a more compendious way of coming at his eſtate. I bought a doſe of poiſon, and prevailed with his cup-bearer, the next time he ſhould call for wine; (which by the bye he drinks with great complacency) to have a ſufficient quantity of the poiſon ready infuſed in the cup. At the ſame time I ſwore a great oath, that, if he ſucceeded to my wiſh, I would not fail to give him his liberty.

ZENOPHANTES.

And pray how did it end? Not as you expected, I ſuppoſe?

[k] Tithonus was ſo handſome, that Aurora fell in love with him, and wiſhed him to live for ever; but, as ſhe was unable, with all her fondneſs, to preſerve him from the infirmities of age, he grew tired of his life, and begged to be turned into a graſhopper; which favour was accordingly granted, and the goddeſs hung him up in the air in a baſket for her amuſement. Tithonuſque remotus in auras. Hor. Od. I. 28. Tithoni croceum linquens aurora cubile. Virg. Æn. 4. 585.

CALLIDEMIDES.

The young man had provided himfelf with two cups againſt our return from the Bath, one for each of us; but, as ill-luck would have it, he made an unfortunate blunder, and gave me the draught, which we had intended for Ptœodorus. He drank his cup, and I mine, which in an inſtant knocked me down dead. Thus Ptœdorus, inſtead of dying himſelf, had me for his proxy. Pray, Sir, what do you laugh at? Is this your behaviour to laugh at your friend?

ZENOPHANTES.

How can I help laughing? A very pleaſant circumſtance, Callidemides, upon my word! But what did the old man ſay?

CALLIDEMIDES.

At firſt he was a little confounded with an accident ſo unexpected. But no ſooner was he recovered from his ſurpriſe, and made acquainted with the man's miſtake, than he laughed as heartily as you do.

ZENOPHANTES.

You should have been contented to let things proceed in the usual train; which, though slow, might have been more sure.

TERPSION AND PLUTO.

TERPSION.

HERE I am dead at the age of thirty, while old Thucritus, upwards of ninety, is suffered to be still alive! Do you call this fair, Pluto?

PLUTO.

Yes, very fair, Terpsion: Why should not he, who never prayed for the death of any friend, be permitted to outlive you, who were perpetually plotting against both his life and estate?

TERPSION.

And pray do not you think, that such an old fellow as he, past all enjoyment, should take himself decently away, and make room for those that are younger?

PLUTO.

That an old man, paſt his pleaſures, ſhould therefore die, Terpſion, is a law quite new! and very different from the inſtitutes of fate and nature!

TERPSION.

I do not deny that. That is what I complain of. There ought to be ſome regular kind of procedure. The oldeſt ſhould go firſt, and then the next; and ſo on; and not let all reaſon and order be reverſed in the manner they are. Only conſider, Sir, what it is for a man to live to ſo very advanced an age, with hardly a tooth remaining in his head, almoſt quite blind, obliged to be carried from place to place, with blear eyes and dropping noſtrils, a living ſepulchre, no longer ſuſceptible of delight, tireſome to himſelf, and diſguſting to others. Whilſt laughter-loving youth, with all its ſtrength and all its beauty, falls down dead at his feet! This is turning things topſy-turvy, and not leſs prepoſterous than the cart dragging the horſe. Beſides ought not a body to be informed of the exact time when one of theſe old fellows may be expected to depart, in order that

that no more care and pains than are absolutely necessary may be expended upon him?

PLUTO.

Matters, Sir, are ordered with much greater propriety than you are willing to suppose. Why should you and such as you be always gaping after other men's possessions? If an old fellow happens to be without children, cannot you let him be quiet, without adopting you? People may very well laugh, when they see you thus disappointed. The more eagerly you wished to be left behind, the more every one rejoices at seeing you go first. Your manner of falling so desperately in love with the old and the ugly, is considered as something new, and affords matter of speculation. It is observed, that those only who are without heirs are the objects of your regard, whilst for those who have you profess no such violent affection. Indeed, many elderly persons, of the latter kind, being not unacquainted with your character, carefully conceal their fondness for their children, pretending even to hate them, that they too may have lovers and be courted. Meanwhile they have no intention at all of allowing these their satellites a place in their last will, in which,

which, as is truly most fit, nature and their own offspring are sure to prevail; and which accordingly produces the most cutting mortification.

TERPSION.

Yes, indeed, I most readily subscribe to what you say. How much of my substance did Thucritus devour, while he seemed every moment at his last gasp! I never entered his house, but he seemed to be coughing up his lungs. And therefore, as I thought it impossible for him to be long out of his coffin, my business, you know, was to take care, that no rival should supplant me in his favour by sending more costly presents. But behold! whilst I lay sleepless on my bed, counting imaginary wealth, and settling every thing just as I would have it, watching and anxiety have been the death of me! Thucritus, it is true, swallowed my bait, but he could not be caught. He attended my funeral the other day, and was not a little diverted on the occasion.

PLUTO.

O rare Thucritus! May you live, old boy, as long as you can, rolling in riches, and laughing

laughing at fuch worthy friends. I fhall be
very forry, if all your flatterers do not die before you.

TERPSION.

I cannot but fay, Pluto, that it would be a
comfortable thing to fee Chariades here.

PLUTO.

Give yourfelf no concern about that. Phidon and Melantus, and every man of them,
will die before Thucritus: their cares will kill
them, as yours did you.

TERPSION.

On thefe terms I am contented. Long life
to you, Thucritus!

[168]

PLUTO [*l*] AND MERCURY.

PLUTO.

DO you know old Eucrates, the childless Eucrates? He is not only very old, but very rich, and thousands are hunting after his estate.

MERCURY.

You mean the Sicyonian. What have you to say of him?

PLUTO.

What I have to say is this. He is now fourscore and ten, and I beg he may be allowed to double his present age at least. I intreat you to grant me this favour; and that you would not fail to dispatch young Charinus and Damon, and the rest of his flatterers, in due order, as fast as possible.

[*l*] So many dialogues on the same subject, hardly differing from each other in any thing material, seem to want some excuse; though none appears to have been made by the commentators, except the prevalency of the custom censured. According to Lactantius, there was no imaginable meanness, no vice however unnatural, to which the candidates for another man's estate would not descend.

MER-

MERCURY.

You make a strange request.

PLUTO.

I know not how strange it may appear, but I am sure it is no more than just. What crime has he committed, that they should be constantly praying for his death? Or, what pretence can they have to his estate, who are not the least akin? But they have taken their leave of all virtue and consistency. As they appear to the publick, they are the most obedient humble servants of a man, whom in their hearts they wish in his grave, the sooner the better. If he is sick, every body is witness to the councils they hold, and the mighty promises they make the Gods, in case of his recovery. In short, this devoted service of theirs is a very odd business; and I most heartily wish that Eucrates may live, and his sycophants depart this life disappointed.

MERCURY.

The ridiculous puppies will richly deserve their fate. Eucrates, for that matter, knows very well how to make the most of them and

their

their hopes. You would think him at death's door, but he is a great deal stronger and more likely to live than most young men are. Notwithstanding they have already parted his estate amongst them, and are growing fat with the prospect.

PLUTO.

I give my hearty consent, that the old man, like [m] Iolaus, grow young again. And let the rascals die in the bloom of expectation, according to their merit, leaving to others their visionary riches.

MERCURY.

Enough said, Pluto. I will take care to send them down to you in proper order, one after another; I think there are seven of them.

PLUTO.

Secure them all. His youth shall be renewed, and he shall live to see an end of them.

---

[m] Iolaus, when very old, was restored to youth by the interest of Hercules. Ovid. Met. 9. 398.

MERCURY AND CHARON.

MERCURY.

IF you please, Mr. Ferryman, we will reckon up how much you are in my debt, that we may have no occasion to quarrel about it hereafter.

CHARON.

I have no objection, Mercury. Let us settle it; it may save trouble.

MERCURY.

You commissioned me to purchase you an anchor, for which I paid [n] five drachmæ.

CHARON.

It was very dear.

MERCURY.

By Pluto, Sir, I gave all the money! I could not get one for less. And I paid a [o] couple of oboli for the leathern thong, to secure the oars.

[n] Three shillings and two-pence three-farthings.
[o] Two-pence half-penny ¾.

CHARON.

Well, put down five drachmæ and two oboli.

MERCURY.

You wanted a large needle to mend your sail: for that I paid [*p*] five oboli.

CHARON.

Put it down.

MERCURY.

For pitch to caulk your vessel, and for nails, and rope for your sail-yard, two drachmæ all together.

CHARON.

Very well; that was a bargain.

MERCURY.

I cannot think of any thing else; though it is very possible something or other may have slipped my memory. When do you say you will pay me?

CHARON.

At present, Mercury, it is impossible: trade is so dead. But who knows? a war or a pesti-

---

[*p*] Six-pence one farthing ¼.

lence

lence may bring us better times. In which case I may have an opportunity now and then in a crowd of making a little money by charging a passenger more than his due.

MERCURY.

That I may get my bill paid, I believe it will be best for me to sit down, and instantly pray for all manner of calamity to fall on mankind.

CHARON.

There is no other way for you to expect your money, I assure you. In this time of profound peace, you see, hardly a soul comes near us.

MERCURY.

For that matter, there is no question, that peace is better for mankind than war, though I am kept out of ready cash by it.—You have not forgot, Charon, the looks of our old customers formerly. They were the men, who used to come to us covered with blood and wounds. Times are strangely altered in our memory. At present one is poisoned by his son, another by his wife; a third dies of a dropsy, the effect of good living. All of them

seem

seem miserable wretches, not in the least like their forefathers. Very many, I am afraid, assassinate one another, to obtain money.

CHARON.

Yes, that same money is a most desireable thing.

MERCURY.

If you think so, you cannot take it much amiss, that you find me rather urgent on this occasion. I only ask for what is my own.

MENIPPUS, AMPHILOCHUS, AND TROPHONIUS.

MENIPPUS.

I Should be very glad to know, [*q*] Trophonius and [*r*] Amphilochus, how it has hap-

---

[*q*] Trophonius had a cave in Bœotia, of so peculiar a property, that whoever had once been in it was never observed to laugh all his life after. Hence it became a proverb, when a person had any thing remarkably sour in his aspect, to say, he looked as if he had just come out of Trophonius's cave. See an account of cures performed by it, Spectator, No. 599.

[*r*] Amphilochus had divine honours paid him at Oropus, a town on the confines of Attica and Bœotia.

pened,

pened, that you two dead men have been dignified with temples, and how you come to pafs for prophets? Nay, the world is even filly enough to fuppofe you a couple of Gods.

AMPHILOCHUS.

If the bulk of mankind be made up of fools, I hope we are not anfwerable for it.

MENIPPUS.

Yes, you are; becaufe the opinions, which they entertain, are no other than the confequences of your cunning. When alive you were dealers in myftery, you pretended to peep into futurity, and refolve the queftions of thofe who confulted you.

TROPHONIUS.

Look you, Mercury; Amphilochus is to anfwer for himfelf, as he thinks beft. For my part, I have only to obferve, that I am a hero, and of courfe a prophet. Whoever comes down to me to confult an oracle, is in no danger of being difappointed. You never can have been at Lebadia, or you would not be fo incredulous.

MENIPPUS.

What, I fuppofe, unlefs I go to Lebadia, and make a fool of myfelf, by creeping on my
hands

hands and knees into a den, wrapped up in linen, with a cake in my hand, I cannot fee that you are as much dead as myfelf, not a bit better than any one of your neighbours, except in the article of lying!—But I beg one thing of you, and conjure you, prophet as you are, not to refufe me an anfwer. Pray what is a hero? for I never could find it out.

TROPHONIUS.

A hero, Sir, a hero is a kind of a compofition, a fort of mixture of man and god.

MENIPPUS.

Something, I underftand, that is neither the one nor the other, but both at once. Pray now where may your better half, your divinity, be at prefent?

TROPHONIUS.

In Bœotia, Menippus, where it utters oracles.

MENIPPUS.

That is not quite fo clear to me. One thing however I am very certain of, that you are dead every inch of you.

PLUTO; a complaint against Menippus.

CRŒSUS.

REALLY, Pluto, there is no enduring this Menippus. Either dispose of the dog somewhere else, or we must absolutely shift our quarters.

PLUTO.

What harm can he do you? He is dead as well as yourselves.

CRŒSUS.

We cannot indulge ourselves in bewailing what is past, without his impertinent interruption. Here is Sardanapalus, who cannot help now and then lamenting the loss of so much good living, any more than Midas and I of our gold and treasures; mean while it is very hard for us to be jeered, abused, and called names by him. He sings, he derides, he disturbs our lamentations. In short, Pluto, he is a very troublesome fellow.

PLUTO.

What is this, Menippus, which they say of you?

MENIPPUS.

What they say, Pluto, is very true: I do not deny it. I hate such mean miserable wretches. Was it not enough for them to pass their lives in the sorry manner they did, but, now that they are dead, they must be hankering after their old pursuits? I despise such fellows, and delight in tormenting them.

PLUTO.

But you should not do so. They have reason to complain. Only consider what they have been obliged to leave behind them.

MENIPPUS.

What, are you turning fool too, Pluto? Do you wish to encourage them?

PLUTO.

No; but I wish you be at peace one with another.

MENIPPUS.

Know then, ye beggarly souls of [s] Lydians, [s] Phrygians, and [s] Assyrians, that I will

[1] Terms of reproach. Slaves were commonly Syrians, Lydians, or Phrygians.

never

never have done despising you! Wherever you go, I will follow you on purpose to plague you. I will laugh at you. I will make songs of you.

CRŒSUS.

Is not this shameful?

MENIPPUS.

No. But your behaviour has been very shameful. You wanted to be adored as Gods. You made sport of your betters, and never once considered how it would fare with yourselves at last. Now all is over; and all I wish you, is to weep your fill.

CRŒSUS.

How vast! how various, ye Gods, were my possessions!

MIDAS.

What heaps of gold had I!

SARDANAPALUS.

In what luxury did I live!

MENIPPUS.

Well done! O rare! Go on and prosper! KNOW THYSELF is a lesson, gentlemen, which seems in unison with your grief, and you may depend upon it, every one of you, I will never cease singing it in your ears.

DIOGENES AND POLLUX.

DIOGENES.

I CHARGE you, [1] Pollux, the next time you get upon earth, (and, I understand, it is to be your turn to-morrow) if you should chance to see Menippus (you may find him at [a] Cranæum, or [2] Lycæum, diverting himself with the wranglings of Philosophy) I beg you will request of him in my name, provided he has had his belly-full of mirth above, to make haste and come hither, where he will find many things more truly ridiculous. While we remain on earth, our ignorance of the future makes it less easy to say, whether we should laugh or cry. But here can be no manner of doubt. Menippus, who will see as clearly, will laugh as much as I;

---

[1] Castor and Pollux were the sons of Leda, one by Jupiter, the other by Tyndarus; consequently one immortal, and the other not. Castor being killed, Pollux requested of his father Jupiter, that his brother might have half of his immortality. Jupiter consenting, they lived and died every day in turn. Virg. Æn. VI. 121.

[a] A cypress grove near Corinth.

[2] A famous school near Athens.

especially when he observes the condition of the rich and great, where even kings are humble, and no otherwise distinguishable from others than by the bitterness of their lamentation. When they think of what they have been, all their courage dies within them, and their pride is for ever at an end. Remember to say all this, and desire him, when he comes, to put plenty of pulse in his wallet, and [y] Hecate's supper (if he should chance to pick it up,) or an [z] expiation egg, or some such matter.

[y] The Athenians had a very great respect for the Goddess Hecate. Every new moon she was provided with a publick supper at the expence of the richer sort, which, when it was brought to the usual place, used constantly to be carried off by the poor, who gave out, that Hecate had eaten it all up. This was done in a place where three ways met; alluding to the threefold nature of the goddess, who was the moon in Heaven, Diana on earth, and Hecate below. The reason why Hecate was placed in the publick ways, rather than other deities, was ὅτι ἐπὶ τῶν καθαρμάτων καὶ μιασμάτων Θεός, because she presided over piacular pollutions. The abovementioned sacrifices or suppers were expiatory offerings, to move this goddess to avert any evils which might impend by reason of piacular crimes committed in the highways.

Potter's Antiquities.

[z] Eggs, pigs, sulphur, &c. were used by the Athenians to purify their theatres, and places of publick resort.

POLLUX.

I will remember what you say. But how shall I know him? What sort of a looking man is he?

DIOGENES.

He is an old man, with a bald pate, and a cloak richly diversified with patches, so hospitably full of holes, as to be open to all weathers. But that which will easily distinguish him is, that he is always laughing, and nothing else so much excites his mirth as the emptiness and impudence of philosophers.

POLLUX.

By these marks I cannot fail to find him out.

DIOGENES.

Shall I trouble you also with a message to the philosophers?

POLLUX.

By all means; I shall not think it any trouble.

DIOGENES.

I wish you to advise them, in one word, to leave off their learned trifling, to have done with their

their disputes about the universe, to forbear planting [a] horns on one another, or making crocodiles, or puzzling the understanding with enquiries into inexplicable nonsense.

POLLUX.

But what will they think of me? Will they not call me an ignorant, illiterate blockhead, who presume to find fault with what I do not understand?

DIOGENES.

Bid them go hang themselves.

POLLUX.

I will.

DIOGENES.

As to the rich, I would recommend to you, my dear Pollux, to address them in this manner: What is the use, ye fools, of hoarding

[a] The following sophism was usual amongst the stoicks and others: "What you have not lost, you have: you have not lost horns: therefore horns you have." Some late authors having been informed, that "Cæsar and Pompey were both of them horned," think this might give rise to what is said concerning the horns of husbands; a proverb which appears to have been in use as early as the days of Artemidorus. Artem. Oneiro crit. 2. 11.

up so much gold? Your calculations of interest, your adding talent to talent, only serve to torment you. [b] One obolus will suffice; and that, let me tell you, will very soon be requisite.

POLLUX.

I will remember.

DIOGENES.

You may tell the stout and beautiful, such as Megillus of Corinth, and Damoxenus the wrestler, that locks of yellow hair, bright black eyes, florid complexions, strong muscles, and broad shoulders, are things unknown with us. All is dust, and every skull is bare and ugly here.

POLLUX.

I will not forget what you say.

DIOGENES.

I wish you to administer some comfort to the poor, who are so very numerous, and so much dejected. Tell them, they may give over their

[b] The Greeks used to put one obolus (some say two) into the mouth of a dead man, to pay for his passage over the Styx.

weeping

weeping and wailing, for all will be equal here. Here they shall behold the envied rich in a fituation no better than their own. You may tell the Lacedæmonians, if you pleafe, that their prefent manners are a fubject only fit for reproach, and that they are loft in a fink of luxury.

POLLUX.

There, Diogenes, you muft excufe me; I will not have any thing to fay againft my countrymen. But I have no objection to deliver your commands to others.

DIOGENES.

Well, I do not mean to infift on what I find is difagreeable to you. You will not fail to execute my other commiffions.

MARS AND MERCURY.

MARS.

PRAY, Mercury, did you hear Jupiter's threats? How arrogantly, nay, how abfurdly he talks! If I fhould take it into my
head,

head, says he, to let down a chain from Heaven, and you should every one of you hang all your weight at the lower end, you would not be able to move me one inch, do all you could: whereas, on the contrary, I could not only hoist up all you godlins together, but earth and sea along with you, with great ease. I give you this as a specimen of his manner of talking, which indeed is no other than such as you yourself have heard. I do not pretend to say, that he is not more than a match for any one of us singly; but that he should be able to overpower so many of us all together, and that we could not all of us weigh him down, with the earth and sea to help us, is a thing incredible, which nobody shall persuade me to believe.

MERCURY.

Have a care what you say, Mars. This indiscretion of yours may bring us into a scrape.

MARS.

You do not suppose I would venture to say this to any body but you, who, I know, can keep a secret? I am not such a simpleton as that. But really to you I could not help commu‑

municating it; what he said was so truly ridiculous. I remember, it is not so very long ago since Neptune, Juno, and Pallas (no more than three of us you observe) made a sort of insurrection, and laid a plot to seize him, and make a prisoner of him. How he did tremble, and quake, and change colours! and, if Thetis, purely out of compassion, had not called to his assistance the hundred-handed [c] Briareus, as sure as you are there, they would have secured him, thunder and lightning and all. Knowing that, it was impossible not to laugh at his bragging.

[b] When the bright partner of his awful reign,
The warlike maid, and monarch of the main,
The traitor-gods, by mad ambition driv'n,
Durst threat with chains th'omnipotence of heav'n;
Then, call'd by thee, the monster Titan came,
(Whom Gods Briareus, Men Ægeon name)
Through wond'ring skies enormous stalk'd along;
Nor he that shakes the solid earth so strong.
With giant-pride at Jove's high throne he stands,
And brandish'd round him all his hundred hands;
Th' affrighted gods confess'd their awful lord,
They dropt the fetters, trembled, and ador'd.
   Pope's Hom. Il. 1. 398.

MERCURY.

Hush! Sir, Hush! I tell you, it is not safe for you to run on in this manner; nor is it prudent for me to hear you.

JUPITER, ÆSCULAPIUS, AND HERCULES.

JUPITER.

HAVE done, Æsculapius and Hercules! you quarrel like mere mortals; which, you cannot but know, is very unbecoming here at a banquet of the gods.

HERCULES.

I hope, Jupiter, you would not have this quack sit above me?

ÆSCULAPIUS.

Surely. Why should not you give place to your betters?

HERCULES.

Betters, indeed! I say betters! Jupiter, I allow, having struck you with a thunderbolt for your [*d*] wickedness, in a fit of compassion afterwards returned you your immortality: is it for that you give yourself airs?

ÆSCULAPIUS.

Surely, Hercules, your memory is none of the best. What do you think of Mount Oeta? I cannot see any reason why a man burnt with an earthly shirt should pretend to despise thunder and lightning.

HERCULES.

However, I believe, Sir, you will find some small matter of difference in our lives and actions. I, the son of Jupiter, behaved like myself, and laboured incessantly for the emolument of mankind, ridding the world of

---

[*d*] Æsculapius, the disciple of Chiron, was so successful in the practice of physick, that Pluto complained to Jupiter of his doing violence to the laws of nature, in having recovered persons actually dead; upon which Jupiter, thinking it high time, knocked him down with a thunder-bolt.

rascals

rascals and monsters. I do not say, that you have not been of some use. You may, for aught I know, have administered your medicines with propriety; but what then? you are still but a collector of simples, a mere mountebank, many degrees distant from the character of man.

ÆSCULAPIUS.

I am obliged to you. You do not deny, then, that I had some merit in curing your burns. It is not so long ago, when, what with the tunick and the fire, you were reduced almost to a cinder. For my part, I am very willing to confess, that I never had the honour of being the purpled slave of an Omphale. As I never made any attempts to comb wool in Lydia, I never had my awkwardness rewarded with a broken head, given by a golden flipper. Nor do I remember losing my senses, and killing my wife and children.

HERCULES.

I tell you what, Sir, if you do not keep a better guard on your tongue, you shall find your immortality stand you in very little stead. For I will take and toss you out of Heaven with

with such hearty good will, that even [*e*] Pæon himself shall find it a difficult matter to mend the cracks in your skull.

JUPITER.

If you do not immediately leave off disturbing this good company with your impertinence, I will send you both a packing directly. But, to be sure, Æsculapius has a right to sit above you, because he died before you.

XANTHUS and the SEA.

XANTHUS.

TAKE me, O sea; compassionate my sufferings, and put an end to my pains.

SEA.

What is the matter, Xanthus? Who can have made you so mortally hot?

[*e*] See Hom. Il. 5. 401, 899. See also Apollonius Rhodius. Arg. 4, 1511.

XANTHUS.

Vulcan. I am almoſt as dry as a cinder. I am boiling hot.

SEA.

What could Vulcan mean by ſuch conduct?

XANTHUS.

O, I know his motive very well; Achilles was the cauſe. I begged and prayed of that ſame ſon of Thetis to leave off murdering the Phrygians, but to no manner of purpoſe; for he proceeded ſo far as even to choak up my ſtream with their dead bodies. At laſt, pitying the poor wretches, whom he was thus wantonly deſtroying, I collected all my force, and ruſhed upon him, in hopes that the fear of being drowned might incline him to peace: when, behold! Vulcan, who happened to be ſtanding by, fell inſtantly upon me with all the fire he had, with all the flames of Ætna, with every combuſtible he could collect! My elms and my [*f*] tamariſks he has totally deſtroyed! My fiſhes, my poor eels are roaſted alive!

[*f*] See Hom. Il. ♦. 350.

You

You see in what a condition he has left me. I am almost entirely gone in steam.

SEA.

You look hot and flustered, to be sure, as might be reasonably expected; for as blood flows from wounds, so heat is the effect of fire. To tell you the plain truth, I think you are rightly served. Had you no regard for a descendant of mine? no respect for the son of a Nereid?

XANTHUS.

Pray, was I to have no concern for the sufferings of my Phrygian neighbours?

SEA.

And, pray, was Vulcan to be less interested in the cause of Achilles, the son of Thetis?

NEPTUNE and the NEREIDS.

NEPTUNE.

LET the ſtrait, into which ſhe fell, be called from [g] her, the Helleſpont. And do you, Nereids, take the girl's dead body, and carry it to Troas, that the people of the country may bury it.

NEREIDS.

Why ſhould you wiſh that, Neptune? Why cannot we give the ſea her body, as ſhe is to give it her name? Conſidering how cruelly ſhe has been treated by a mother-in-law, we pity the poor girl from our hearts.

NEPTUNE.

What you propoſe [b], Amphitrite, cannot be. It is not proper, for her to lie here in the

[g] Helle, the daughter of Athamas king of Thebes, flying from her ſtepmother, fell off the golden ram, on which her brother Phryxus and ſhe had ventured to ride, in order to croſs the ſtrait between Propontis and the Ægean ſea; which from thence was called the Helleſpont.

[b] Neptune firſt addreſſes himſelf to the Nereids in general, and now to only one. But that one, the reader ſhould remember, is Amphitrite his wife.

ſand.

fand. She shall be buried in Troas, as I said before, or Cherfonefus. And it will not be a great while before she will have the fatisfaction of [*i*] Ino's fuffering as much as she has done, and in the fame manner too. Ino, driven from houfe and home by Athamas, will tumble head-foremoft from the top of Cithæron, with her fon in her arms, into the fea.

NEREIDS.

Ino nurfed and fondled Bacchus. We muft fave Ino, to oblige him.

NEPTUNE.

We cannot refufe doing any thing to oblige Bacchus; but it is more than she deferves.

NEREIDS.

How happened the girl to fall? her brother Phryxus rode fafe enough.

NEPTUNE.

Very well he might. He is a young man, and fits firm in his feat. She, poor thing, underftanding nothing of the matter, found the ram an uncouth kind of vehicle, and was no fooner upon his back, than she was ftruck with

[*i*] Helle's cruel ftepmother.

the aftonifhing appearance of the deep below.
She trembled all over. She grew giddy with
the profpect; and, when fhe could no longer
keep her hold, fhe let go the ram's horns, and
fell plump into the fea.

NEREIDS.

Should not her mother Nephele have affifted her?

NEPTUNE.

Suppofe fhe had, could Nephele contend
with fate?

NEPTUNE and the DOLPHINS.

NEPTUNE.

WELL done, Dolphins! ye are always
friendly to the human race; I will fay
that for you. Formerly ye took up the fon of
Ino when he and his mother fell from the [*k*]
Scironides into the fea, and carried him to the
Ifthmus. And now one of you has not only

[*k*] Rocks hanging over the fea, at the extremity of Cithæron and other mountains in Bœotia.

fnatched

snatched up the harper of Methymna, but carried him bag and baggage through the water as far as Taenaros, the more effectually to save him from the wicked sailors.

DOLPHINS.

You need not wonder at our affection for mankind, since we were men once ourselves.

NEPTUNE.

I think Bacchus might very well have been contented with vanquishing you, as he had done others, without transforming you into fishes after the fight at sea.—But, pray, how was this affair concerning Arion?

DOLPHINS.

[*I*] Periander, it seems, was highly delighted with his playing, and, on that account, would very frequently send for him. In short, after getting money in his majesty's service, he had a mind to go home to Methymna, to shew it. Accordingly he went on board a ship for that purpose, which happened to be manned with

[*I*] Periander, one of the seven wife men of Greece, was the last king of Corinth.

a set of rascals; and, having been indiscreet enough to discover what he carried with him, when they were got to about the middle of the Ægean sea, the sailors fell upon him, with intent to dispatch him. "Gentlemen," says he, (you must know I swam close to the vessel, and heard every word that was said) "Gentlemen," said he, "since such is your pleasure, far be from me to oppose it. I only beg your permission, before I throw myself overboard, in order to save you the trouble, to take up my harp, and sing my own elegy." This was no sooner consented to, than he packed up his alls, gave them a soft tune, and let himself down into the sea, as a dying man. I immediately laid hold of him, put him on my back, and swam with him to Tœnaros.

NEPTUNE.

I admire your taste, who suffered not his sweet notes to perish unrewarded.

MENELAUS and PROTEUS.

MENELAUS.

LOOK you here, Proteus, as to your being turned into water, as you belong to the sea, I can make a shift to believe that. Nay, your becoming a tree, or even a lion on occasion, is tolerable. But to transform yourself into fire, and notwithstanding that to live in the sea, is so very unaccountable, that I must beg to be excused: there is no such thing as believing it.

PROTEUS.

Why should you be so surprised, Menelaus? It is not a whit stranger than true.

MENELAUS.

Nay, for that matter, my own eyes—but I beg your pardon, Proteus. I must own I suspect some legerdemain in the business. Have not you some method of bewitching one's eye-sight, and making us think we see what we do not?

PROTEUS.

I wonder how you can think of any deceit in a thing so evident as not to admit of any? Were not your eyes sufficiently open, when you saw into how many things I metamorphosed myself? However, if you still pretend not to believe, and call it all fancy, I shall only beg the favour of your hand, my good Sir, when I am fire. You will then be able to judge whether seeing be believing; and perhaps your feeling may allow me to possess the faculty of burning.

MENELAUS.

I am not very fond of making the experiment: there may be danger in it.

PROTEUS.

I fancy you have never seen the Polypus. Are you acquainted with the nature of that fish?

MENELAUS.

I cannot say that I have not seen it. But, as to the nature of it, I should be glad to learn that from you.

PROTEUS.

When that fish clings close to a rock, he changes his colour, and takes that of the stone, which he so exactly mimicks, that the simple fishermen believe him to be what he pretends, and pass him by.

MENELAUS.

So they say. But admitting all this, it is a mere nothing to what you do.

PROTEUS.

I cannot so much as guess who will be able to gain credit with a man, who distrusts his own eyes.

MENELAUS.

I have seen it. I own, I have seen it. But it is still most unaccountable to me, that fire and water should be made of the same materials.

The CYCLOPS and NEPTUNE.

CYCLOPS.

OH! father, what I have suffered! That stranger, that villain, who made me drunk, fell upon me when I was asleep, and has put out my eye!

NEPTUNE.

Who could dare to behave so, Polyphemus?

CYCLOPS.

Who? At first he called himself NOBODY. But, as soon as he thought himself fairly out of reach, he roared out lustily, that his name was ULYSSES.

NEPTUNE.

Now I know whom you mean, Ulysses of Ithaca, in his return from Troy. But how came he to do you this injury? I did not think he had been half so stout.

CYCLOPS.

Coming home from the pasture, I caught several persons in my den, who were met there, it was very plain, with no good defign againſt my ſheep. I had faſtened my door with a great ſtone, which I have for that purpoſe, and kindled my fire with ſome wood, which I had brought from the mountain. They, being thus diſcovered, tried to ſecrete themſelves. However, I got hold of ſome of the raſcals, and ſerved them right, making no bones of them. To make them go down, that pretty gentleman, that Nobody, that Ulyſſes, or what you pleaſe to call him, gave me ſomething or other to drink, which was in truth very pleaſant, and had a fine flavour. But it proved moſt treacherous and miſchievous. I drank it up, and very ſoon afterwards every thing ſeemed all at once to be going round and round. My cave was turned topſy turvy, like my poor brain. At laſt I fell faſt aſleep. Upon that he got ready a ſharp ſtake, put it into the fire, and with the [*m*] burnt point of it blinded me as I lay. You ſee in what a condition he has left me.

NEPTUNE.

You muſt indeed, my ſon, have been very faſt aſleep, not to be rouſed with the loſs of

[*m*] Telo lumen terebramus acute. Virgil.

your

your eye! But how did he get off? I am sure Ulysses could never be man enough to remove the great stone from the door.

CYCLOPS.

I took it away myself, thinking I should have a better chance to catch him. And seating myself by the door, to grope for his going out, I determined to let nobody pass me but my sheep, which I committed to the care of the ram, having given him orders accordingly.

NEPTUNE.

I begin to guess, that he was sly enough to get off undiscovered amongst the sheep. But why did not you call the rest of the Cyclops as loudly as you could to come and help you?

CYCLOPS.

I did call, father, and they came, and asked me what was the matter with me. But, when I told them how I had been betrayed and ill-used by Nobody, they directly concluded me not right in my head, and would have nothing farther to say to me.— A designing villain! to impose on me so with his lying name! What vexes me above all the rest, he laughs me to scorn,

scorn, telling me I may rest contented, for it is not in the power of my father [n] Neptune to relieve me.

NEPTUNE.

Be comforted, my son; I will be revenged on him, never fear. Though I cannot cure your loss of sight, I would have him to know, that all those who sail on the seas are in my power. And he has not yet got to land.

PROMETHEUS and JUPITER.

PROMETHEUS.

LOOSE me, I pray, Jupiter; surely I have suffered enough.

JUPITER.

Yes, to be sure! Your fetters ought to be ten times heavier. All Caucasus was full little enough to lay upon your head. You ought to have sixteen hungry vultures all rioting on your liver at once, and your two eyes should

[n] Hom. Od. IX. 525.

be scooped out of your head. Pray, Sir, who was it stole the cœlestial fire? Did not you dare to manufacture that vile animal, man? But why do I talk of man? Did not you make woman? I forbear to mention your scandalous imposition upon me in parting the treat [*]. You thought the greasy bones good enough for Jupiter, and kept all the best to yourself.

PROMETHEUS.

Even supposing my offence to have been whatever you please to represent it, do not you think I have been sufficiently punished? Here have I been fast nailed this long time to this huge mountain, and obliged to find perpetual liver for this accursed eagle!

[*] The ancients having been long accustomed to consume every part of the sacrifice in the service of the Gods, to the great detriment of the poorer sort of votaries, Prometheus interfered in the matter, and obtained a promise from Jupiter, that he would be contented for the future with one half. That ingenious mechanick, having afterwards made an offering of a couple of bulls, when they were cut up, put the flesh in one hide, and the bones in another, and offered Jupiter his choice; who, suspecting nothing, took the bones. However the trick would not pass again, the Gods for the future insisting on the whole.

Hyginus in Astronomico Poetico.

JUPITER.

It is not the thousandth part of what you deserve.

PROMETHEUS.

I do not desire to be set at liberty without making a proper satisfaction: I can tell you something, Jupiter, I believe, which you would be very glad to know.

JUPITER.

What, you want to come round me so, do you? No, no, Sir, I am not so easily outwitted.

PROMETHEUS.

What could I propose to myself by outwitting you? You would be at no loss to find out Caucasus again, and could always have fetters in plenty for me.

JUPITER.

Let me know what service of consequence it is in your power to render me.

PROMETHEUS.

If I should tell you whither you are now going, would you trust my predictions another time!

JU-

JUPITER.

Yes; tell me that, and I will believe you.

PROMETHEUS.

You are going to visit Thetis. I shall not mention your errand.

JUPITER.

It is even so, for certain. Well, and what else can you tell me?

PROMETHEUS.

It is a connection, which I wish you to avoid. If that Nereid should bring you a son, I am pretty well assured, that he would serve his father just as you did yours.

JUPITER.

Dethrone me, I suppose, you mean!

PROMETHEUS.

You may take my word, Jupiter, that I am very far from wishing it; but I wish you to guard against it.

JUPITER.

I will take your hint, and think no more of her. And, for your friendly admonition, Vulcan shall set you free.

CUPID.

CUPID AND JUPITER.

CUPID.

IF I have been guilty of any offence, I hope, Jupiter, you will forgive me; as you see I am a poor little boy, not come to years of discretion.

JUPITER.

A little boy indeed! you are older than [*p*] Iapetus. You are well experienced in every species of mischief. But, because your beard is not grown, nor your temples covered with snow, truly you must pretend to be an infant!

CUPID.

But what harm have I done you, Jupiter? Suppose I am old and crafty, surely I have given you no reason for wanting to confine me?

[*p*] The son of Titan and Terra, and the father of Prometheus. Though the Greeks considered him as the founder of their nation, they did not always think themselves obliged to speak with respect of him, but used to call any old fellow, who had outlived his faculties, Iapetus.

Cupid, according to Hesiod, is the most ancient of the Gods. Theog. 120.

JUPITER.

You little villain! you have given me reasons in abundance. Have not you made a fool of me a thousand times over? You have done with me whatever you pleased. You have metamorphosed me into a satyr, a bull, a shower of gold, a swan, an eagle, and every thing else that is ridiculous. I may well say ridiculous, for I never had a mistress that entertained any real regard for me. All your art in that has proved insufficient. To stratagem and disguise I owe all I can boast. As a bull or a swan they may endure me; but should Jupiter declare himself openly, they would all be ready to drop down dead with fear.

CUPID.

No wonder of that. What mortal can bear the aspect of Jove?

JUPITER.

How did Branchus and Hyacinthus endure Apollo?

CUPID.

Apollo need not brag; for all his fine hair and his smock face, Daphne ran away from him.

him as fast as her legs could carry her. But I will tell you what, Jupiter; if you wish to be liked by the women, you must not go shaking that [*q*] ugly shield of yours; nor rattling about your frightful thunder. Make yourself as pretty a fellow as you can. Do up your hair in the most elegant taste. Hang down a curl on each side of your head. Wear a fine bonnet over your locks. Get a purple coat, and a pair of embroidered slippers. Trip lightly along to the sound of the pipe and the timbrel. Do this, and you shall soon have admirers more in number than the Mænades of Bacchus.

JUPITER.

Pshaw! Do you think I would purchase love on any such terms?

CUPID.

Then you must live without love; that is all.

[*q*] Jupiter's shield, or ægis, so called from being covered with the skin of the goat that suckled him, had on it the figure of a Gorgon's head, with curling serpents instead of hair, so terrible as to turn all beholders into stone.

JUPITER.

No, not so neither; but I can purchase it at an easier rate. Go, go, get you gone.

APOLLO and VULCAN.

VULCAN.

PRAY, Apollo, have you seen Maia's hopeful brat? He is a mighty fine child, it seems; smiles on every body, and promises fair, they say, to turn out something very extraordinary.

APOLLO.

A fine child! do you call him? He may turn out something very extraordinary, I grant you, for in mischief he is already as old as the oldest.

VULCAN.

He cannot have done any mischief as yet, for he is but just born.

APOLLO.

Neptune, whose trident he has stolen, I believe, will tell you a different tale. Or, if you enquire of Mars, you will find that his sword has been conjured out of the scabbard. I need not mention myself: he has only robbed me of my bow and arrows.

VULCAN.

Surely it cannot be? Why, Sir, he can hardly turn himself in his cradle.

APOLLO.

I do not desire you to take my word for it. If he should come your way, you may satisfy yourself.

VULCAN.

He has done that already.

APOLLO.

Has he? and have you all your tools? Have you lost nothing belonging to your shop?

VULCAN.

No. I have lost nothing.

APOLLO.

Be sure? Look again.

VULCAN.

As I am here, my tongs are gone!

APOLLO.

You may chance to find them in the baby-cloaths. That is the likelieſt place.

VULCAN.

How nimble-fingered he is! Why, Sir, he muſt have ſtudied thieving in his mother's womb!

APOLLO.

And his tongue is not leſs nimble than his fingers; ſo that he thinks of being engaged in the ſervice of Apollo. Yeſterday he challenged Cupid to wreſtle a fall with him, and tripped up his heels in the twinkling of an eye. While Venus was careſſing him for it, he took the opportunity to rob her of her ceſtus. And while Jupiter was laughing and enjoying the jeſt, he made free with his royal ſceptre; and, if the thunderbolt had not been ſomewhat of the heavieſt, as well as too hot to hold, he would have carried off that too.

VULCAN.

A forward child! I muſt needs confeſs.

APOLLO.

Then he is a dab in muſick too?

VULCAN.

How does that appear?

APOLLO.

From a very fine inſtrument, which he made of a dead tortoiſe that he happened to find. He made handles and fitted a neck to it, which he furniſhed with pegs. He made the bridge. He put ſeven ſtrings to it. With this [r] inſtrument he makes ſuch elegant, ſuch exquiſite muſick, that even I, an old, an experienced harper, cannot but envy him. Beſides, you muſt know, that his mother ſays, he cannot bear to be in heaven at night, his curioſity carrying him down to hell, for the greater conveniency of pilfering. He is furniſhed with wings for expedition, and has contrived for

---

[r] The moſt ancient lyres were made of the ſhell of a tortoiſe; which, as an amphibious creature, may be called indifferently piſcis or fera. Without taking this into conſideration, it is not eaſy to underſtand ſeveral paſſages in the ancient poets. See Spence's Polymetis, p. 107. Statius i.5. Hor. iv. 3. &c. The lyre of Polyphemus, as Lucian informs us in the dialogue between Doris and Galatea, was made of the ſkull of a ſtag. Allan Ramſay mentions a fiddle conſtructed from the " harn-pan of an umquhile meer."

himself a very extraordinary [s] rod, with which he drives about the poor ghosts, and manages the dead just as he pleases.

VULCAN.

[t] I gave him the rod for a play-thing.

APOLLO.

And he has rewarded your generosity: witness the Tongs.

VULCAN.

Well remembered! I will go and search the cradle for them.

VULCAN AND JUPITER.

VULCAN.

WELL, Jupiter, what is to be done now? I am come, as you ordered me, with an ax sharp enough, if you should have occasion to cleave a stone in two.

---

[s] See Hom. Od. 5. 47. translated by Virgil. Æn. 4. 242.

[t] According to Servius, Apollo had this rod before Mercury, which he gave to the latter, in exchange for a lyre. See Servius on Æneid 4. 242.

JUPITER.

You have done right. Down with it, and cleave my head in two.

VULCAN.

Do you take me to be out of my senses? Do, pray, Jupiter, in good earnest tell me what it is you would have me to do.

JUPITER.

I do tell you, that I want you to lay open my skull. Perhaps you may choose to refuse me this favour: if you do, you may chance to remember it. Come, Sir, do your business immediately, and with a hearty good-will. Strike home, I tell you. What I feel in my brain is enough to distract a body.

VULCAN.

Yes; but let us beware of doing more harm than good. The ax is extremely sharp, and you will not find it a very delicate midwife.

JUPIDER.

Do not you trouble your head about that. Leave the consequence to me. Strike, I tell you.

VUL-

VULCAN.

Nay, for that matter, there is no refusing you; if I must, I must. Heyday! as I am here, a young lady in armour! Indeed, indeed, Sir, your head might very well ach, and you had some pretence to be out of humour with this terrifick wench preying on your pia mater! Your shoulders had a camp rather than a head to support. O rare! she dances the Pyrrhick dance! She is inspired, to be sure! Only mind how she tosses about her shield, and brandishes her spear. What is most extraordinary, she is already a full-grown beauty. How her helmet sets off her blue eyes! As I have been your midwife, I hope, Jupiter, you will give me the maid for my pains.

JUPITER.

For my part, I assure you, that I should have no manner of objection; but she is resolved on perpetual virginity, and it cannot possibly be.

VULCAN.

Let me but have your consent, and leave the rest to me. I warrant you, I shall have her.

JUPITER.

You have my leave to catch her if you can. But I know it to be a thing impracticable.

NEPTUNE and MERCURY.

NEPTUNE.

MERCURY, may a body fpeak with Jupiter?

MERCURY.

By no means, Neptune.

NEPTUNE.

However, you may tell him of my being here furely?

MERCURY.

But indeed I may not, and I defire you not to be troublefome. He is not at leifure, and you cannot fee him at prefent. It is not convenient.

NEPTUNE.

Is he with Juno?

MERCURY.

No; he has an engagement of quite another kind.

NEPTUNE.

Ganymede?

MERCURY.

No, no; he is not well.

NEPTUNE.

Not well! how so? you astonish me.

MERCURY.

I am almost ashamed to say it; but so it is.

NEPTUNE.

Nay, surely you may tell me your uncle?

MERCURY.

My uncle then must know, that at present Jupiter is in the straw. He lies-in.

NEPTUNE.

Pish! how came he with child? I desire to know who is the father. What! has he been all the while an Hermaphrodite, without our knowing any thing of the matter? He did not discover

discover any symptom, I think, of growing bigger than usual in the waist?

MERCURY.

No: that was not the place.

NEPTUNE.

Oh! now I understand. His head has had another delivery. Upon my word, that same pate of Jove's is very prolifick.

MERCURY.

Yes, his head produced Minerva; but he was taken in labour this time in his thigh, in which he had deposited the babe of Semele.

NEPTUNE.

O rare! there is no barren soil about Jupiter! But, I pray you, who is Semele?

MERCURY.

Semele was a Theban, one of the daughters of Cadmus, and with child by Jupiter.

NEPTUNE.

One might have expected her to bring forth, I think, rather than him.

MERCURY.

However ſtrange and unaccountable the matter may appear to you, it is as I tell you. You are no ſtranger to Juno's jealouſy of him; and ſhe is as ſly as ſhe is jealous. She prevailed upon poor ſimple Semele to requeſt of her gallant, that he would viſit her in all his pomp and parade of thunder and lightning. Jupiter reluctantly conſented, and agreed to go to her like himſelf. But behold! in a moment the houſe was on fire, and the poor woman periſhed in the flames. As ſhe was ſeven months gone, Jupiter ordered me to cut her open, and bring the child to him. Which I had no ſooner done, than he put the embryo into a hole in his thigh, which he had made for that purpoſe, and where it continued its proper time. It is now the third month ſince that was done, and he has been juſt brought to bed, and is as well as can be expected.

NEPTUNE.

And where is the child?

MER-

MERCURY.

I have taken him to the Nymphs of Nyſa, who are to bring him up. His name is Bacchus.

NEPTUNE.

So he has father and mother both in one!

MERCURY.

Yes. But fare you well. Till Jupiter gets up again, I muſt be nurſe, and ſee that he wants nothing.

※※※※※

JUPITER and the SUN.

JUPITER.

YOU worſt of the Titans, what a piece of work have you made! You have deſtroyed every thing upon earth. You have given up your chariot to the guidance of a fooliſh boy, and the conſequence has been ſuch as you might very naturally have expected. He has burnt up every thing on earth, and every where elſe all nature is ſtarved with cold.

In

In short, this hopeful charioteer of yours has thrown the whole syftem into confufion; which if I had not obferved in time, and let fly a thunderbolt at his head, which knocked him down, I dare fay, he would have made an end of mankind, and not left one remaining.

SUN.

I acknowledge, Jupiter, that I have done wrong. But, pray do not be fo very angry. I was not prevailed upon till after much intreaty; and then it was to pleafe my own dear boy. And, befides, how was it poffible for me to dream of fuch terrible confequences.

JUPITER.

So then you did not know what a hopeful bufinefs you fet him upon! You, to be fure, were ignorant, that the fmalleft deviation from the ufual track was nothing lefs than utter deftruction! Could you be fo much unacquainted with the difficulty of managing fuch fpirited fteeds, and what a tight rein they require? You know very well, that, if you give them their heads, though but for a moment, there is no fuch thing as recovering the command

of

of them. A plain proof of which is, that the poor unfortunate lad has been dragged by them all manner of ways, to the left, and to the right, backwards and forwards, upwards and downwards; meanwhile he was unable to do any one individual thing to help himself.

SUN.

I knew it all full well, and very loth I was to give up the point. But he made such a sniveling, such a begging and praying, with his mother Clymene to second him, that I found it a thing impossible not to comply. At last, when I could not hold out any longer, I consented to his mounting my chariot, not without many admonitions and a great deal of good advice. I assured him of the necessity of keeping himself firmly fixed in his seat. I told him how far, in going up hill, he might let the horses have their heads. I then directed him the way downwards, and charged him to keep a tight rein, and curb their impetuosity to the utmost of his power. I pointed out to him the great danger of going the least wrong. The boy (and truly one could expect no less) was no sooner seated, than he was frightened out

of his senses at seeing himself ride with such a
fire, and beholding such an immense space below him. The horses, presently learning to
despise their new driver, flew headlong out of
the road; and then followed all the mischief.
He immediately let go the reins, and, in order
to save himself from falling, seized fast hold
with both his hands on the [s] round of the
chariot. Alas! he has met with the punishment of his rashness; and I am sure, Jupiter, I have had vexation enough about it!

JUPITER.

Do you think then his punishment has been
half enough? However, I am contented for
the present to overlook what is past. Only let
me advise you to beware of a similar offence.
If ever you presume hereafter to employ such
another deputy to do your business, a thunderbolt shall very soon make you sensible of the
difference between your fire and mine. As to
the boy, let his sisters take and bury him where
he fell, on the banks of the Po. Their tears

[s] ἄντυξ, to which the reins were occasionally fastened.
See Hom. Il. v. 262. Phaeton's conduct was just of a piece
with his, who lays hold of the mane of a run-away horse.

shall be turned into amber, and themselves into poplar trees. Do you take care and get your chariot repaired (I understand the pole is broken, and one of the wheels damaged); and put to your horses, and go on with your business as usual. Mind what I say to you.

OF SACRIFICES.

IF any man of tolerable sense were to take into his consideration the sacrifices, the feasts, the processions made to the Gods by his silly brethren; what they pray for, what they wish for, and what sentiments they entertain concerning their several deities; he must be in a very grave humour indeed, if he did not smile at such monstrous absurdity. But truly, before he indulge himself in his mirth, it may well become him honestly to enquire whether such a kind of devotion deserves the name of piety, or whether such wretched votaries are not in reality at enmity with the gods, whom they thus represent in so mean and beggarly a light as to stand in need of human aid, to be

tickled

tickled with flattery, and piqued at being neglected. All the misfortunes of Ætolia, the distresses of Calydonia, the wasting away of [*t*] Meleager, and many other murders, were all owing, it seems, to the anger of Minerva, who, being forgotten in the sacrifices of Oeneus, found herself grievously affronted. So terribly she took it to heart, that I imagine I see her this moment solitarily moping in heaven, while every body else is gone to enjoy a good dinner! How she frets, when she thinks of it! On the other hand, supposing Jupiter to have

[*t*] Me'eager was the son of Oeneus and Althæa. Oeneus was king of Calydonia. When Meleager was newly born, his mother heard the Fates, who sate by the Fire, say the child should live till that billet, which one of them held in her hand, was consumed. Upon which they departed, and presently the mother extinguished the stick, and laid it carefully up. When he was grown, his father, sacrificing to the Gods after harvest, forgot Diana, who thereupon sent a prodigious boar to destroy his lands; which the young man seeing, got some assistance, killed him, and presented his head to Atalanta, the daughter of Jaseus, king of the Argives, who had given the boar the first wound. His uncles by the mother's side were so angry at this, that they wanted to take away the head from the princess; which he opposing, slew them, and married her. His mother on this flew into a passion, and burned the billet; and at the same time Meleager died. See Ovid. Met. viii. 270.

any

any gratitude for favours received, how happy
may the Ethiopians be supposed to be, who,
as Homer informs us in the first book of his
Iliad, feasted the God and all his friends for
twelve whole days together! Those deities, it
seems, are prudent dealers, and part with nothing without a valuable consideration: if men
want any thing good, they must even be contented to pay for it. Health, for example,
may be purchased for a heifer; riches for four
bulls, a kingdom for a hundred, a safe return
from Troy to [u] Pylos for nine, a fair wind
from Aulis for a virgin princess. Hecuba gave
[x] Minerva a dozen cattle, and a veil for her
vote and interest to defer the taking of Troy.
Things of less consequence, as it is but fair,
are sold at a less rate, and given in exchange
for a cock, or a garland, or a snuff of incense.
Old Chryses, the priest, having studied divinity,
knew all this very well. When he returned
from Agamemnon, without having been able
to effect his design, " Apollo," says he, " I
must needs say, that I think you have some
slight obligations to me, which it would very

[u] Not so cheap, according to Homer, who makes the
sacrifice to Neptune nine times nine. Od. iii. 7.
[x] Hom. Il. vi. 274.

well become you to repay. Your Temple might have remained without a chaplet to this hour, if I had not bestowed that honour upon it, which, you know very well, I have done repeatedly over and over again. Recollect yourself a little. How many fat thighs of bulls and goats do you think I have roasted on your altars? And are all my services to pass for nothing? And does Apollo totally disregard so good a friend as I have been to him?" Upon this speech Apollo grew so heartily ashamed of himself, that he instantly snatched up his bow and arrows, and posting himself on an eminence near the harbours, he thence scattered pestilence and death amongst the poor Greeks, who perished in heaps, together with their dogs and mules. Since Apollo is come in my way, I shall take occasion to mention some other particulars, which are told of him by learned men. I do not mean to insist on his having been unfortunate in his amours, the haughty disdain of Daphne, or the death of Hyacinthus. I shall just mention his being sentenced, for the murder of the Cyclops, to be banished from Heaven, in consequence of which ostracism he was glad to put up with the lot of mortality upon earth.

earth. In Theffaly he had but homely fare, being retained as a hired fervant by Admetus; as he was in Phrygia by Laomedon. When he lived with the latter, Neptune was there alfo in the fame capacity. They were both of them very glad to be employed as Bricklayers labourers; but had the misfortune to be bilked by their mafter of a very confiderable part of their wages, to the amount, as I have been told, of above thirty Trojan drachmas. And yet how pompoufly the poets always talk of the Gods, In what magnificent ftrains do they defcribe the characters of Vulcan, and Prometheus, and Saturn, and Rhea, and indeed Jupiter's whole family! Having firft of all invoked the aid of the Mufes, and feeling the divine inflation, they ftraightway fing, as they fhould do, how Saturn, having made an eunuch of his father Cœlus, reigned in his ftead; and how he afterwards eat up his own children, like the Argive Thyeftes; how Jupiter, by the cunning of Rhea, who contrived to wrap up a ftone in his place, efcaped being fwallowed, and was expofed in Crete, where he was nurfed by a goat, as Telephus was by a doe, and Cyrus of old by a bitch; how he dethroned and imprifoned his

father,

father, and then set up for himself; how he married a vast number of wives; and last of all Juno his sister, according to the licence of the Eastern customs; that, being quite dissolute and abandoned in his amours, he soon filled all heaven with the fruits of them; some of which indeed might be very well entitled to that honour, but many others were mere bastards, begotten on mortality; how my gentleman, to carry on his intrigues, assumed a greater variety of shapes than even Proteus himself, sometimes condescending to become yellow gold, sometimes a white swan, sometimes a bull, sometimes an eagle; that he had one child begotten, conceived, and born of his brain; how he snatched another out of his mother's womb, when she was about half gone, the house being on fire, and herself perishing in the flames; that he deposited the babe in a hole in his thigh, where it throve very well, and of which he was delivered at the proper time, and with the usual pains of child-birth. They report things not less strange concerning Juno, who, as they say, was got with child by a breeze of wind; by which curious commerce alone she was enabled to bring forth Vulcan. Vulcan is

not

OF SACRIFICES. 233

not the moſt lovely babe in the world, being nothing better than a poor mechanick, a dirty tinker, a mere [*y*] fire-ſtone, envelloped in ſmoke, and burnt black with the fire of his own ſhop; over which he conſtantly ſtands, and of courſe is all over ſoot and cinders. He had a moſt terrible fall given him by Jupiter, who took and toſſed him headlong out of Heaven; which makes him ſo lame. Indeed, if the Lemnians had not very good-naturedly interfered and broken his fall, it had been all over with him, and Vulcan had been as effectually knocked down dead [*z*] as Aſtyanax. But this is all nothing. Every body knows how Prometheus was ſerved merely for his extraordinary affection for mankind. Jupiter took him into Scythia, and crucified him, in a manner,

[*y*] Πυρίτης a pyrite, a fireſtone. Grævius can by no means conceive any propriety in this, and therefore finds fault with the tranſcribers for corrupting the text. As if a blackſmith might not be called a pyrite by the ſame figure of ſpeech which allows a dull commentator to be called a log!

[*z*] Aſtyanax was the ſon of Hector. After the deſtruction of Troy Ulyſſes threw him headlong from the top of a tower, that no one man might be left to revenge the cauſe of his country.

upon

upon Mount Caucasus, where he was bound
fast for the purpose of having his liver eaten
up every day of his life by an eagle. Such was
the revenge which he took on Prometheus. As
to Rhea (I suppose a body may speak) I really
wonder she is not ashamed of herself. Such
an old worn-out Harridan as she, the mother of
so many Gods, to be hankering after young
fellows at her time of life! She constantly accompanies her Attis in her chariot drawn by
Lions, not willing to trust him out of her sight,
though he be no longer an object of jealousy.
And after this who can blame Venus for her intrigues with flesh and blood? Or, who can find
fault with Dame Luna, if she now and then
descends from her Orb, to visit her dear Endymion?—But it is time to have done with such
talk as this. Let us mount up to Heaven with
Homer and Hesiod, and see what is to be seen
there. The outside is of brass. So said Homer
long ago. Going higher, if you bend back
your head, or rather lie down with your face
upwards, the light appears so much the brighter,
the sun becomes more refulgent, the stars more
distinct, the whole firmament is glittering gold,
the universe a blaze of day. The Hours, who
live

live at the entrance, are the porters; next to them are Iris and Mercury, servants and meſſengers of Jupiter; next comes Vulcan's ſhop, furniſhed with all manner of tools; then the habitations of the Gods, and the palace of Jove ſupreme. So far all is prodigiouſly fine, being the workmanſhip of Vulcan [a]. The deities, ſeated by Jupiter (here would it well become me to exalt my ſtyle) hang down their heads, caſt their eyes upon earth, and keenly dart their glances round, if haply they can any where eſpy a fire kindled to convey the aſcending volumes of well-ſeaſoned ſmoke. If they find any body offering ſacrifice, they fall to work immediately with open mouth, feaſting greedily on the ſume. If blood is ſpilt upon their altars, they are as buſy, ſucking it up, as ſo many flies. If they ſup at home, nectar and ambroſia is the word. Mortals formerly have been admitted to their table; but ſince Ixion took it into his head to be rude to Juno, and Tantalus became a tell-tale, they are not only to this day ſufferers themſelves for their impertinence, but have proved the means of

[a] Οι δι Θιοι παρ' Ζηνι καθημενοι. Il. iv. 4.

excluding

excluding every body else from such great company. Such is the life of the Cœlestials; which men have been contented to follow at humble distance. These latter have consecrated groves, and mountains, and birds. To each divinity has been assigned his own particular tree. The Gods are divided into nations, and their votaries are enrolled accordingly. Apollo is the God of Delos and Delphi. Athens acknowledges Minerva, as is denoted by the name [*b*]. Argi has Juno, and Mygdon Rhea, and Paphos Venus. The Cretans not only insist upon it, that Jupiter was born and brought up in their island, but they go so far as to shew his grave. And we had all the while been grosly imposed on, in taking it for granted, that Jupiter rained, and thundered, and performed many other notable exploits; never once imagining, that the honest fellow had been a long time dead and buried in Crete! That the Gods may not be without house and home, temples are built. Meanwhile Praxiteles, or Phidias, is employed in taking a likeness. Where these ingenious artists ever saw any of their originals, I cannot say; but

---

[*b*] Αθηνα, Minerva; Αθηναι, Athens.

they

they always take care to reprefent Jupiter with
a beard, Apollo ever young, Mercury juft arrived at manhood, Neptune with dark hair, and
Minerva with blue eyes. When you enter the
temple, you are not left to fuppofe, that what
you behold there is ivory, brought from India,
or gold dug out of the mines of Thrace, but
the true identical fon of Saturn and Rhea; Phidias having been pleafed to bring him down
with him from Heaven, and given him orders
to refide on earth, where he is to fuperintend
the dreary [*c*] Pifa, and to reft himfelf contented with an occafional offering once in five
years. After erecting altars, preparing incan-
tations, and getting ready the [*d*] fprinkling

[*c*] A diftrict of Elis, in Peloponnefus, to which belonged
the city Olympia and the river Alpheus, famous by the Olympick games and the temple of Jupiter Olympius.

[*d*] περιρραντηριον was a veffel (ufually of ftone or brafs) filled
with holy water, with which all thofe that were admitted to
the facrifices, were befprinkled, and beyond which it was
not lawful for any one that was βεβηλος, or profane, to pafs.
Potter's Antiquities, vol. I. p. 189. La Cerda in a note on
Virg. Æn. vi. 230, Spargens rore levi, &c. fays, Hence
was derived the cuftom of Holy Church, to provide puri-
fying or holy water at the entrance of their churches. See
Dr. Middleton's Letter from Rome.

tubs,

tubs, men produce their respective victims. The plowman brings his fellow-labourer, the ox; the shepherd a lamb, the goatherd a goat: One offers frankincense; another a cake. The poor man makes his peace by kissing his hand. But let me not pass over the manner of performing sacrifice. The animal, having been first strictly examined, that he may be as perfect as possible, is crowned with a garland, and conducted to the altar, where he is slaughtered before the eyes of the God. While this is doing, the creature sends forth a certain dismal note, which, I suppose, is to be considered as something propitious, being a lower-toned kind of accompanyment suited to the business. Surely the Gods cannot fail to be delighted with such sensible doings! Whoever has defiled his hands, is strictly enjoined by a written tablet, not to think of going beyond the vessels of Lustration. The priest, all over bloody, stands by like another [*e*] Polyphemus, intent upon

[*e*] When Ulysses arrived in Sicily, Polyphemus, the Cyclops, seized him and his companions and carried them into his cave, where he eat up a couple of them. Ulysses afterwards, having contrived to make him drunk, took the advantage of his being asleep, and bored out his eye, his only eye, with a firebrand. See Hom. Od. 9. Virg. Æn. 3.

business.

business. With all the pious care imaginable he cuts up the animal, tears out the entrails, pulls out the heart, and sprinkles the blood upon the altar. Last of all, lighting his fire, he takes the sheep or goat, and broils it in the skin or wool, all together. The sacred fume, so worthy of the God, ascends on high, and is gradually dispersed all over heaven. Amongst the Scythians such pitiful victims are held in contempt, and they offer men in sacrifice, being well persuaded, that nothing less considerable will appease their patroness Diana. So far all is moderate, and much of a piece with what is transacted in Assyria, in Phrygia, and Lydia. But, if ever you should travel as far as Ægypt, there indeed you may see something to claim your reverence, something more than common. Jupiter there has the head of a ram, Mercury looks for all the world like a dog, and Pan is neither more nor less than a goat. There too are to be seen the Ibis, the Crocodile, and the Ape.

[f] Then, if thou be resolved on knowing all,

[f] Hom. Il. vi. 150. and Il. xxi. 487.

a thou-a thousand sophists and scribes, and bald-pated prophets will tell you, after the preface of "Hence, hence, ye profane!" that, dreading the insurrection of the Giants and other enemies, the Gods took sanctuary in Ægypt; where, in order to be more secure from the danger of being discovered, one of them assumed the shape of a goat, another that of a ram, this became a beast, and that a bird, as every one's fears and fancy inclined him. For this reason it is, that these several forms are continued to this day, being carefully deposited in the sacred recesses of their temples, as they were described in Hieroglyphicks [g] ten thousand years ago. There is hardly any thing particular in an Ægyptian sacrifice, except their sorrow for the victim. They stand round it as it expires, and beat their breasts with every token of concern. Sometimes it is buried immediately after being killed. Their principal God is Apis. When he happens to die, the publick grief is without all bounds. On so melancholy an occasion who can set any value on the hair of his head? Though a man had the

[g] The modern Chinese go far beyond the ancient Ægyptians in their pretences to Antiquity. See Voltaire and others.

purple

purple lock of [b] Nisus, he would shew it no
mercy, but cut it immediately off, and expose
his bald head filled with affliction. The most
beautiful and most respectable beast in the
herd is selected with all diligence, and appointed to succeed the deceased God. All this,
which is the general belief and practice, is too
absurd for censure; though Democritus could
not but laugh at the folly, while Heraclitus
must weep for the ignorance of mankind.

[b] Nisus, king of the Megarensians, had a purple lock, on
the preservation of which depended that of his kingdom. Notwithstanding which, Scylla his daughter, being in love with
his enemy Minos, cut it off, and gave it to him. Nisus died
with grief, and was changed into a hawk, as she was into a
lark. Hence, they say, arises the enmity between these birds.
Ovid. Met. viii.

THE SHIP; or, THE WISHES.

LYCINUS, TIMOLAUS, SAMIPPUS, and ADIMANTUS.

LYCINUS.

I KNEW very well how it would be. A savoury carcase lying in the open air would sooner escape the eye of a vulture, than any strange sight could fail of the observation of Timolaus! Why, Sir, you are so very curious, that, were there any thing new, though as far distant as Corinth, you would run thither to see it without once drawing breath!

TIMOLAUS.

What would you have had me to do, Lycinus? I had heard of this immense vessel being arrived at [i] Piræus, at a time when I had nothing else to engage my attention. It is one of the vessels employed in bringing corn out of Ægypt into Italy, and an extraordinary one it

[i] A port of Athens.

is. I dare say, the only errand you and he had out of the city was to see it.

LYCINUS.

You do not guess much amiss. Adimantus also of [*k*] Myrrhinus came with us, but we have lost him somewhere in the crowd, and I cannot imagine what is become of him. We all came together to the ship, and went aboard together; first you, Samippus, then Adimantus, and then I, having fast hold of him with both my hands. As I had shoes on, and he had none, he handed me up the steps, and from that moment to this I have never been able to set eyes on him, neither aboard the ship, nor any where else.

SAMIPPUS.

If you recollect, we lost him immediately after that handsome young fellow came out of his cabbin. You remember the young man with the fine linen, who had his hair tied behind, and made to lie back from each side of his forehead. If I know any thing of Adimantus, I presume he had his reasons for giving the slip

[*k*] A town of Attica.

to our Ægyptian hoſt, who ſhewed the curioſities of the ſhip.

LYCINUS.

The young man was paſſable enough. But Adimantus muſt have acquaintance at Athens better ſuited to his taſte. That youth, beſides his being of a dark complexion, has thick lips, and is ſpindle-ſhanked. Then he drawls and minces his words in ſuch a manner, that his foreign pronunciation eaſily betrays him to be no native of Greece. His manner alſo of twiſting and turning back his hair beſpeaks him of mean birth.

TIMOLAUS.

Amongſt the Ægyptians, Lycinus, that betokens a quite contrary diſtinction. The young gentry of that country dreſs their hair in that manner from boys; juſt as our anceſtors uſed to do when advanced in years, binding it up on the top of the head with a golden [/] graſhopper.

[/] See the Scholiaſt on Ariſtophanes, Clouds, 980. See alſo Thucydides, near the beginning of his firſt book.

SAMIPPUS.

You are in the right, Timolaus, to remind us of what Thucydides has written in his preface concerning our ancient luxury, and that of our old friends the Ionians.

LYCINUS.

Now, Samippus, I call to mind where it was that we left Adimantus. While we stood staring at the maft, counting the impreſſions on the [m] hides, admiring how nimbly the failors ran up the ropes and acroſs the fail yards, laying hold with their hands—then it was we loſt him.

SAMIPPUS.

You are right. It muſt have been then. But what ſhall we do? Are we to wait here for him? Or, would you have me go back to the ſhip.

---

[m] Leather and ſkins of beaſts were applied to ſeveral uſes; as to cover the ſcalmi, and the holes through which the oars were put out, to preſerve them from being worn. There were ſkins under the rowers, called ὑπηρεσία, and ſometimes, ὑπαγωνια, ἱστοργα τῷ ϛενῷ, from ſaving the elbows or breeches of the rowers. Scheffcri Mil. Nav. p. 140.

TIMOLAUS.

By no means. Let us go on, I beg of you. Very likely, when he could not find us, he might make the best of his way home, and pass us in his hurry. If not, Adimantus knows his way very well, and there is no danger of his being lost.

LYCINUS.

I am afraid it may prove an unfortunate circumstance for us to leave our friend in this manner. But however, if Samippus is of the same opinion as you, why, let us even go.

SAMIPPUS.

I am for going on by all means, provided we have any chance of finding the palæstra open.—Only think what a ship! The carpenter declared she was a hundred and twenty cubits in length, and above thirty in breadth; and from the deck to the deepest part of her hold, where the pump is, twenty nine. And then what a prodigious mast! and what a sail-yard

it

it has to support! what [n] stays she has! how the [o] stern stands, gradually bending with the golden [p] gosling! Opposite to which, rising in due proportion, stands the prow, shewing on each side the Goddess Isis, the ship's namesake. The paintings, the red flag, the anchors, the windlass, the contrivances for turning round, the stowage, the cabbins, all the decorations are truly admirable! And then what an army of Mariners! Her cargo of corn was said to be enough to feed all Attica for a twelvemonth;

[n] Πρόλοι were cords, which, passing through a pulley at the top of the mast, were tied on one side to the prow, on the other to the stern, to keep the mast fixed and immovable. Scheffer.

[o] The πρυμνα, or stern, was of a figure more inclining to round than the prow, the extremity of which was sharp, that it might cut the waters; it was also built higher than the prow, and was the place where the pilot sate to steer. Scheffer.

[p] Χηνισκος was so called from χην, a goose, the figure of which it resembled, because geese were looked upon as fortunate omens to mariners, as they swim without danger. This ornament, according to some, was fixed at the bottom of the prow, where it was joined to the foremost part of the keel; and was the part to which anchors were fastened when cast into the sea. But others carry it to the other end of the ship, and fix it on the extremity of the stern. Scheffer.

all which was in the custody of a little old fellow, who managed the immense helm with an inconsiderable twig of a handle. Heron, I think, was his name. I saw his head, part of which was bald, and the rest curled.

TIMOLAUS.

His companions all pronounced him a most extraordinary sailor, excelling even Proteus himself in the knowledge of whatever relates to the sea. I suppose you have been told how he conducted the vessel to her port, as well as what happened in the voyage, and how the people on board were saved by a star?

LYCINUS.

No; but I should be very glad to hear.

TIMOLAUS.

I had it from the honest pilot himself, who is very communicative. He told me they sailed from Pharos with a moderate gale, and within seven days were in sight of Acamas; then, a west wind coming full in their teeth, they tacked and came to Sidon. Ten days after, having passed by [*q*] Aulon, they arrived at the Cheli-

[*q*] A town on the coast.

donean iflands, after they had narrowly efcaped going all to the bottom in a moft violent ftorm. I know very well by experience what a dreadful fea runs there, and efpecially in a fouth-weft wind. At a little diftance is the parting of the Lycian and Pamphylian feas. The breaking of the many waves on the promontory, fome of which rife to an enormous height, makes a tremendous noife, and occafions the fharp and craggy appearance of the rocks. They were juft on the point (he faid) of being dafhed againft thefe rocks in the night, in a difmal dark night; when the Gods, fubdued by their wailings, fhewed them a fire in Lycia; fo that they could plainly diftinguifh the coaft, and at the fame time a bright ftar on the top-maft head, where one of the twins had taken his ftation, in order to direct the veffel to the left into deep water, juft in time to prevent her ftriking. Falling down from thence with a direct courfe, they croffed the Ægæan fea; and, on the feventieth day from their leaving Ægypt, with the trade-winds againft them, they yefterday got to Piræeus, being carried fo much too low. Whereas, if they

had

had kept Crete on their right, as they should have done, and gone above [r] Malea, they would have been in Italy by this time.

LYCINUS.

Upon my word, a moſt admirable pilot this ſame Heron! His courſe reſembles that of a ſea-god rather than a ſailor [s]. But who goes yonder? Adimantus?

TIMOLAUS.

It is indeed Adimantus, and no other. Let us call to him. Holla! Adimantus! Adimantus, the ſon of Strobichus, of Myrrhinus, Holla!

LYCINUS.

Either he is in a pet, or elſe he has loſt his hearing; for I am ſure it is Adimantus, and

---

[r] A promontory of Laconia.

[s] Τῳ Νηρεϊ ἐλαύνοντι, ἐς τοσουτον ασφαλη της ὁδυ, equal to Nereus for going out of the way. Martinus du Soul ſays, he cannot tell what Lucian means here, or why he ſhould drag in Nereus. Nereus, every one knows, was a god of the ſea, who may therefore be ſuppoſed under no neceſſity of ſailing with a fair wind, nor very anxious about reaching a port on the coaſt.

nobody

nobody elfe. I fee him very plainly. It is his
drefs, his gait, and he is fhaved, as ufual, to
the very quick. Let us mend our pace, and
try to overtake him.—Why, Adimantus, unlefs
a body lay hold of your coat and ſtop you,
there is no poſſibility of making you hear. You
ſeem buried in thought, and it muſt needs be
a buſineſs of no ſmall confequence, which can
ſo totally engroſs your attention.

ADIMANTUS.

Nothing bad, Lycinus. Only, as I was coming along, a new conceit came into my head,
which took ſuch entire poſſeſſion of me, that
I proteſt I never heard you till this moment.

LYCINUS.

If it is not a very great ſecret, I hope you
will tell us what it is. Beſides, we have been
initiated in the myſteries, as you very well
know, and conſequently have been taught the
art of holding our tongues.

ADIMANTUS.

You will think it ſuch a childiſh thought,
that I am aſhamed to mention it.

L Y-

LYCINUS.

Some love-affair, perhaps? We are not such strangers to the tender passion, that you should scruple making us your confidants.

ADIMANTUS.

Pshaw! no such thing. I had formed in my imagination the Island of Bliss; and, when you two came up, you surprised me on the summit, in the utmost excess of riches and pleasure.

LYCINUS.

We are come then very opportunely to cry halves! You can do no less than produce your stores. We are your friends, Adimantus, and you must allow us to partake with you.

ADIMANTUS.

I placed Lycinus where he was safe, and immediately after found myself left. It was almost the very moment we got aboard. While I was busy taking measure of the anchor, you had slipped away without my observing it. After my curiosity was satisfied in other respects, having seen every thing I could, I enquired

quired of one of the failors, how much profit the ship might generally bring to the owner, upon an average, one year taken with another. [*t*] Twelve Attick talents, he told me, at the lowest computation. Upon this, as I was returning home, it came into my head, that, if some propitious deity would but make me the owner of this vessel, I should not only be very happy myself, but able to serve my friends. Sometimes, said I, I will sail in her myself, and sometimes send my deputies. I directly quitted the house, which I inherited from my father, by the river Ilyssus; because, with the twelve talents (only one year's freight of my ship), I could very well afford to build another in a much better situation, a little above the Pæcile. The next thing I did was to buy slaves, and fine cloaths, and chariots, and horses. Then I put to sea, and was the admiration of every one on board my ship. My sailors considered me as very little less than a king, and stood in awe of me accordingly. But, behold! while I was making preparations to enter the

[*t*] The greater Attick talent contained 80 minæ; which makes the value of twelve such in English money 3100*l*.

port, which was juſt appearing in ſight, Lycinus unluckily came up. I was going right before the wind, and altogether as my heart could wiſh, when you turned my veſſel topſy-turvy, and ſunk my poſſeſſions in the ſea.

LYCINUS.

If that be the caſe, no doubt you will make me appear before my betters to anſwer for myſelf as a pirate, infeſting the highway between Piræeus and the city, where you have juſt ſuffered ſo terrible a ſhipwreck. But hold—let me give you a little comfort in your affliction. Why cannot you, if you pleaſe, have in a minute five veſſels all handſomer and larger than that you have loſt; and, what is ſtill better, not one of your new ones ſhall be liable to ſuch an accident? Every one of the five ſhall arrive from Ægypt five times every year richly loaded with corn; which will of courſe make ſo great a man as the owner moſt intolerably ſaucy. For, if it was ſo difficult to obtain an audience when you had but one, what can be expected when you come to be maſter of five more, of [*n*] three ſails each, and none of

[*n*] Very large.

them

them in any danger of sinking? You will not so much as vouchsafe to bestow a look on an old friend. And so, Sir, I wish you a good voyage! We will wait in the port, and enquire of those that may chance to touch there from Ægypt or Italy, whether any body has been so fortunate as to obtain a sight of the great Isis of Adimantus.

ADIMANTUS.

There! I was very certain that I should only be laughed at! But I can stay till you are gone, and put to sea again. I had much rather be busy amongst my sailors, than be laughed at here by you.

LYCINUS.

I beg your pardon. We mean to accompany you on board.

ADIMANTUS.

Do you? Then I will step on before, and take away the ladder.

LYCINUS.

Then we will try what swimming will do. Since it is so very easy for you to become pos-
                                                            sessed

fessed of so many stout vessels without either buying or the trouble of building, why should it be thought a mighty matter for us to obtain of the Gods the faculty of swimming as far as we please without the least fatigue? It is not such a great while ago, you know, that we went all together to Ægina to the rites of Hecate, in a little thing of a boat, at the rate of four oboli apiece. We were then very good friends, and you had no manner of objection to our company. Why then should you pretend to take it so much amiss, that we wish to go aboard your vessel with you, that you talk of going on before and taking away the ladder? This ship of yours makes you forget yourself, Adimantus. And your fine new house, built in so lovely a situation, together with the number of your attendants, makes you not a little vain. However, Sir, notwithstanding all this, I hope you will not forget to favour us with some slices of salt fish, when your Isis returns from Ægypt. Or, suppose you were to treat us with a box of Canopian perfume, or bring us over the Ibis from Memphis. Pray, Sir, if there be room in your

hold

hold, could not you oblige us with one of the pyramids?

TIMOLAUS.

A truce with your wit, Lycinus: you make the gentleman blush. You have handled his veſſel in ſuch a manner, that ſhe is all over leaky, and no longer in a condition to keep the ſea. But come, ſince we are yet at a great diſtance from the city, let each man of us take his ſhare of the way, and implore the Gods immediately to beſtow upon him whatever he likes beſt. By which means we ſhall be ſo little ſenſible of fatigue, that our journey will be a pleaſure to us, every one being a volunteer in the buſineſs, and enjoying his dream juſt as long as he pleaſes. We will not ſuppoſe the Gods at all unwilling to grant whatever we ſhall think fit to aſk, however unnatural or unreaſonable. So that the boundary of every man's wiſh will be only his own ſovereign will and pleaſure. There will be this great advantage in it, that we ſhall ſee who is diſpoſed to make the beſt uſe of proſperity; ſince it will be juſt the ſame as if he were in real poſſeſſion, and rich to all intents and purpoſes.

SAMIPPUS.

I am quite of your mind, Timolaus; and, when it comes to my turn, I shall be ready to wish for myself. As to Adimantus, he is one half on board, and we may leave him out of the question. But what says Lycinus?

LYCINUS.

O let us all be as rich as you please: I am not the man to envy the common felicity.

ADIMANTUS.

Who shall be the first to begin?

LYCINUS.

You, Adimantus; and after you Samippus; and then Timolaus. I shall begin within half a furlong of [*] Dipylon, and get on as fast as I can

ADIMANTUS.

Before I think of stirring from my ship, let me amend my petition. So may Mercury, tho

---

[*] The principal gates of Athens were the Πυλαι Θριασιαι, afterwards called Διπυλον, because they were larger than any of the rest. They were placed at the entrance of Ceramicus, and therefore seem to have been the same with the πυλαι Κεραμικαι. Potter's Antiquities.

god

god of Gain, be propitious! Let me have the ship with all her cargo! The merchandize, the passengers, the women, the sailors, and every thing else, if any thing else remain that is desirable, I wish all to be mine!

SAMIPPUS.

Do not forget your being on board.

ADIMANTUS.

I suppose you mean to put me in mind of the boy. Well, let me have him too! and let all the wheat be turned into gold, a * darick for every grain!

LYCINUS.

You do not want to sink your vessel, I hope. Surely you do not consider what a difference there is in the weight between wheat and gold.

ADIMANTUS.

Do not you be so envious, Lycinus. When it comes to your turn, you shall wish for Mount [y] Parnes in solid gold, if you like it, without a word from me.

---

* A darick was worth about eight shillings.
[y] A mountain of Attica, famous for its vineyards. Parnes benignus vitibus. Statii Theb. 12. 620.

LYCINUS.

Nay, Adimantus, do not be angry: I meant nothing more than to provide for the safety of the ship and crew, which, I was afraid, might be carried to the bottom by such a prodigious weight of metal. Not perhaps that you are in so much danger. But that lovely youth—he cannot swim.

TIMOLAUS.

Give yourself no uneasiness on that account, Lycinus. The Dolphins will take care of him, and carry him safe to land. They saved a [z] harper, you know, for an old song. Another

[z] Moses du Soul says, this is meant of Amphion. It is strange how very ignorant in little things great men often are! The most profound of all modern Philologists is of opinion, that salt is apt to melt in hot weather. See a late annotator on Shakespeare's King Lear, Act IV. Scene 8. De Arione consule Plinium Hist. Nat. 9, 8. cujus testimonio omnes antiqui consentiunt. Nec diversa canit Robertus Lloyd:

    The sailors, people not r.nown'd
    For nice intelligence of sound,
    Chuck'd poor Arion fairly o'er
    To swim at least nine leagues to shore.

ther [a] young man was very civilly conveyed by them after his death to the Isthmus of Corinth. And would there be no fond fish, do you think, to take under his protection the new domestick of Adimantus?

ADIMANTUS.

I see, Timolaus, you are determined to outdo Lycinus in raillery on this occasion, though you yourself so seriously introduced the subject.

TIMOLAUS.

Would it not have been better to order matters so, that the treasure might have been found under your bed; which would have saved you the trouble of getting your gold out of the ship, and afterwards having it to carry into the city?

> Down fiddle went, and fiddler—pish!
> He got a horseback on a fish!

Mr. Lloyd confined in the Fleet to Mr. R. confined in the Gout. The epistle thus begins:

> There is a magick in sweet sounds,
> Which calls forth every thing but—pounds.

[a] Melicerta. See Ovid's Met. iv.

ADIMANTUS.

You are right, perfectly right, Timolaus. So
let there be a thousand bushels of gold coin
dug up from under the statue of Mercury,
which stands in the [b] area. First of all, as
old [c] Hesiod advises, let me think of my
house; which, I am resolved, shall be most
sumptuous. Whatever is about the city shall
be immediately mine; all belonging to the [d]
Isthmus, to Delphi, and Eleusis. I must have
all the seacoast; and some part of the [d] Isthmus, for an occasional residence during the celebration of the games. The plains of Sicyon,
whatever is well wooded and watered, whatever is fertile in Greece, let all be instantly

---

[b] Where his bed was.
Lectus genialis in aula.   Ep. Hor. i. 1. 87.

[c] Οικον μεν πρωτιστα, γυναικα τε, βουν τ' αροτηρα,
  Κτητην ο γαμετην, ητις και βουσιν εποιτο.

First of all provide yourself a house, then a wife, then an ox,
then a plowman, then a servant-maid, to tend your cattle.
Hesiod's Works and Days. ii. 23.

[d] There is something aukward and embarrassed in the
original here, owing probably to blunders in transcribing.

mine.

mine. I do not intend to eat or drink out of any think less precious than gold. Do not tell me of such pitiful cups as those of Echecrates: I will not have one of mine to weigh a grain less than two talents.

LYCINUS.

But where do you propose to find a butler strong enough to hand you a bumper? Or, how would you be able to receive from him such a cup as it would puzzle Sisyphus himself to hoist up?

ADIMANTUS.

None of your impertinence? I tell you, Sir, my tables shall be of solid gold, and my beds the same. If you say another word, I will have my servants gold too.

LYCINUS.

I hope at least, that you will be a little more considerate than Midas was, and not have your meat and drink of gold; lest you should fall a victim to your own desires, and be starved with hunger in the midst of so much wealth.

ADIMANTUS.

Be so good, Sir, as to reserve your stock of prudence for your own use, and let me with as I like best. My cloaths shall be of purple, my eating the most elegant, my sleep most sweet. My friends shall approach me with the utmost respect, to present their humble petitions. Struck with awe, what man will do less than adore me? Clænetus and Democrates, and many others who carry their heads very high at present, shall have an opportunity of cooling their heels at my gate in a morning. They will come forward, no doubt, very confident of being admitted to my presence before any body else; but I shall give orders to my seven lusty [*e*] barbarian porters to bang the door full in their faces, as a proper sample of their own good manners. To certain others, whenever it shall so seem meet, I will rise lowering, like the sun in a cloud, not so much as condescending to let them look in my face. In the mean time, if a poor man (such as I once

[*e*] See Pliny's Nat. Hist. xi, 16.

was myself) should meet my observation I will treat him with the utmost politeness, and invite him to dine with me. How do you imagine those fellows, who now think themselves rich, will feel themselves, when they see my chariots, my horses, my swarms of beautiful attendants; all in the flower of their age? Do not you think, they will die of envy? My dinners shall be all served in gold: Silver is by no means becoming a man of my rank. I will have my saltmeat and Oil from Iberia, my wine from Italy. My honey shall not be smoaked: I will have my provisions, my boars, my hares, my birds from all parts of the world, fowls from Phasis, peacocks from India, cocks from Numidia. All my caterers and cooks shall be the greatest adepts in their art. When I drink, whoever pledges me shall carry off cup and all. Those who are now esteemed rich shall be no more than beggars in comparison of me. Dionicus, I fancy, when he sees my very domesticks rolling in silver, will hardly be so proud of shewing his cup and his little dish. The city shall be honoured with the following privileges: to every citizen each month, I will distribute

diftribute a [g] hundred drachmæ, and fifty to
every inmate. I will fpare no expence in publick
buildings: the theatres and baths fhall be adorn-
ed with exquifite art. I intend to bring the fea
to Dipylon, and to have a harbour fomewhere
thereabouts; to effect which I muft firft have
a monftrous great ditch made to convey the
Water. My fhip may then come up fo near,
as to be very plainly feen from the Ceramicus.
I fhall not forget to be liberal to my friends.
To Samippus, for inftance, I have ordered my
fteward to meafure out twenty bufhels of gold
ready coined, to Timolaus [h] five pints; to
Lycinus one, and that barely meafure, becaufe
forfooth he cannot keep his tongue within his
teeth, but muft be making game of my wifh.
This is the life I propofe to lead, being rich
beyond meafure, wallowing in luxury, and enjoying every pleafure to the utmoft. I have no

[f] Three pounds four fhillings and feven-pence.

[g] χοινξ, here tranflated a pint, is equal to one pint, 15,7
Inches. It was the ufual allowance of victuals and drink,
which a Grecian Houfekeeper allowed each of his fervants
for a day.

more

more to fay, nor any more to afk of Mercury, of whom, I only beg, that he will be punctual.

LYCINUS.

You are not to learn on what a flender fecurity your wealth depends. It hangs by a little, little thread; and, when that breaks, all is gone.

ADIMANTUS.

What do you fay?

LYCINUS.

I fay, my good Sir, that nothing can be more uncertain than the duration of your riches. Suppofe yourfelf juft fitting down to your golden table; before you can extend your arm, before you can tafte your peacock, or touch your Numidian fowl, you may chance to breathe your laft, and leave your fine dinner for the crows and vultures. It would not be a fingular cafe; for I can produce feveral inftances, if you have any mind to hear me, of perfons dying in circumftances exactly fimilar, while others have lived to fee themfelves ftripped of all they poffeffed by fome envious
demon

demon or other. The sudden fall of Crœsus and Polycrates, men much richer than you, and of which you must have often heard, are cases in point.—But, not to insist on this, were I to allow that your riches may last, how are you sure that your health will continue, without which you can have no satisfaction in any thing? You see many of the rich living in torment: some have lost the use of their limbs, and are unable to walk: Some are blind, and others complain of intestine disorders. I know very well, without asking you, that you would not wish to be such a fop as Phanomachus, though you were to be master of twice as much. I need not trouble you with a [i] repetition of the plots, the thefts, the envy, the odium, which are the constant companions of wealth. Only consider what a deal of trouble you are like to have.

[b] The reader, who feels himself disgusted with the repetition of idle remarks, is not to lay them at the door of the translator, who has a sufficient number of his own offences to answer for.

ADIMANTUS.

You are always against me. I tell you what, Lycinus, at the rate you go on, you may chance to come short of the pint of money, which I promised to give you.

LYCINUS.

Then you will act just like the rest of your wealthy brethren, in going back from your word, and not regarding what you say. But it is your turn now, Samippus.

SAMIPPUS.

I am an Arcadian, you know, a native of Mantinea, and must not be expected to wish like a man who lives near the coast. I do not defire a ship; for if I had one, I could not have the pleafure of shewing it to my neighbours. Nor do I mean to haggle with the Gods in meafuring me out gold and treafure. As every thing is alike eafy to them, and they are not to refufe us whatever we may afk (for fo Timolaus faid, when he propofed this wifhing, begging of us not to baulk our fancies), I will even wish to be a king. I do not mean such an one as Alexander the son of Philip, or Ptolemy, or Mithridates, or any other who succeeded to a kingdom by right of inheritance. I wish to advance myself by degrees. First of all let me have about thirty good fellows, in whom I can confide, to assist me in raising [i] contributions on the publick. I would then have their number increased by the accession of three hundred more, which may afterwards gradually rise to a thousand, and, in good time, amount to ten times the number. In short, I would have in all about fifty thousand men with heavy armour, and five thousand horse. Being then appointed to the supreme power by the free suffrages of all, from my superior merit in the

[i] What the Greeks called Ληστεία, the Latins Latrocinium, and the English Grand Larceny, was the first step towards being a finished hero. See the ancient Historians passim.

   Servetur ad imum
 Qualis ab incepto processerit. Hor.
A good beginning makes a good end.

arts of negociation and government, that circumſtance, you ſee, gives me a great advantage over other kings, as my exaltation is owing to my virtue only; and I do not riſe to greatneſs merely becauſe I am the inſignificant heir of another man's acquiſition. That kind of ſucceſs is much akin to the riches of Adimantus. But there is no authority half ſo pleaſant as that which a man is conſcious of having put himſelf in poſſeſſion of.

LYCINUS.

So, Sir, you are determined to run away with all the prime part of the wiſhing! To have the command of ſo many armed men, to be the unanimous choice of fifty thouſand people, is in truth no ſmall matter. We were ignorant before, that Mantinea could boaſt of having bred ſo admirable a king, who is at the ſame time ſo great a general. Come, Sir, give us a ſpecimen of your power, command your army, fit out your cavalry, marſhal your troops. I long to know what unhappy country, what devoted people, ſo many Arcadian heroes mean firſt to invade.

SAMIPPUS.

I will tell you, Lycinus. Or, had you not better go with us yourself and fee? I will give you the command of five thousand horse.

LYCINUS.

I am greatly honoured, Royal Sir, and, after the Perfian manner, can do no lefs than dutifully to hang down my head, with my hands behind my back, paying all proper deference to your diadem, and not forgetting the ftarchnefs of your tiara. However, I muft intreat you to beftow the command of your cavalry on fome ftouter man. For my part I have very little relifh for the fervice, having never once been on horfeback in all my life. And I fhould be dreadfully afraid, on founding to arms, of tumbling off and being trod under foot in the crowd. My fpirited fteed, champing his bit, might take it into his head to rufh on with me amongft the thickeft of the enemy; in which cafe, I apprehend, unlefs I were tied faft to my faddle, I fhould foon lofe my rein and my feat too.

ADIMANTUS.

Let him take the command of the right wing; and I will lead on the cavalry, Samippus. I presume on your having presented me with so many bushels of money, and can hardly bring myself to think that you will refuse me any thing.

SAMIPPUS.

I believe, however, there would be no impropriety in asking them the question, whether they would wish to be under your command. All you gentlemen of the cavalry, who wish to be commanded by Adimantus, hold up your hands! They are unanimous in their choice of you, you see. Do you, therefore, Adimantus, take charge of the horse; and let Lycinus have the right wing, and Timolaus the left. I myself will occupy the centre, according to the manner of the [k] Persian monarchs, when they con-

[k] The kings of Persia would accept of nothing less than actual adoration as a condition of being spoken to. Ælian has a story of a Theban ambassador, who, to avoid giving offence, and at the same time preserve the dignity of the country he came from, contrived to drop his ring in the royal

condescend to grant an audience. Let us now
advance over the mountains towards Corinth,
first invoking the aid of Jove, propitious to roy-
alty. As soon as we shall have subdued all
Greece (which we shall do without being once
engaged in fight, since nobody will think of
opposing us) we shall put our horses into ferry
boats proper for the occasion, and go ourselves
on board gallies (there being plenty of corn in
[*l*] Cenchreæ, and shipping, and every other necessary provided beforehand) in order to sail
over the Ægæan sea into Ionia. There, after
sacrificing to Diana, we shall find no manner of
difficulty in taking the unfortified towns, in
which we will appoint our governours, and
proceed through Caria into Syria. From thence
we shall pass into Lycia and Pamphilia, and Pi-
sidia, and the high and low Cilicia, till at
length we arrive at the Euphrates.

royal presence, and in picking it up went through the
preliminary act of adoration, which consisted in bending
the back and hanging down the head. V. H. i. 21.

[*l*] A town in the Isthmus of Corinth.

LYCINUS.

Suppose, royal Sir, you make me Lord Lieutenant of Greece. I am not fond of going so far from home as you talk of, nor have I any great stomach for fighting. I suppose you will march against the Armenians and Parthians, those warlike nations, so famous for their skill in aiming the deadly arrow. For which reason I shall be as well satisfied, if you will assign to some other my command of the right wing, and leave me your [m] Antipater behind you in Greece. I could not be all over iron and steel, and, in leading on your phalanx for you, some mischievous arrow or other about Susa or Bactra would certainly shoot me.

SAMIPPUS.

You would not be a coward, I hope. Do not you know, Sir, that to quit your post is a capital offence? Since we have now got to the river Euphrates, over which we have thrown

[m] Antipater was the name of one of the Captains of Alexander.

a bridge of boats, taking good care to leave all
secure in our rear, by my prudent appointment
of a viceroy over each conquered nation, I have
thought fit to dispatch proper persons to reduce Phœnicia, Palestine, and Ægypt. First
of all, Lycinus, do you pass the river with the
right wing. I will follow, and after me Timolaus. Adimantus, with the cavalry, shall bring
up the rear.—In marching through Mesopotamia no enemy has ventured to look us in the
face. They have very readily given up both
their citadels and themselves. Advancing to
Babylon, we got within the walls, you see, and
take possession of the city before the inhabitants are aware of us. The king, who passes
his time chiefly at Ctesiphon, hearing of our
invasion, goes to Seleucia, and prepares to re-
pulse us, by raising all his horse, and sum-
moning immediately his whole body of archers
and slingers. We have intelligence from our
spies, that an innumerable army is already assembled, eager for battle, two hundred thousand of which use the javelin on horseback.
We are further informed, that neither the Armenians, nor those about the Caspian sea, nor
the Bactrians, are yet arrived; but that the
whole

whole of this amazing force is made up of perfons near the city, and in the king's own neighbourhood. So very powerful he is, and fo ready and numerous are his refources. And now, I think, it begins to be time for us to look about us.

ADIMANTUS.

I think fo too. And I am further of opinion, that you of the infantry fhould march directly to Ctefiphon, while we, the horfe, ftay here to defend Babylon.

SAMIPPUS.

You do not like to be in the neighbourhood of danger, Adimantus. What do you fay, Timolaus?

TIMOLAUS.

I fay, that our beft way will be to go directly againft the enemy, with all the forces we are able to mufter, and not to wait till they be joined by fuch prodigious numbers as are flocking to them on all fides. Let us fall upon them in their march immediately, before their auxiliaries can get up.

SAMIPPUS.

You speak like a sensible man. What do you think, Lycinus?

LYCINUS.

I will tell you what I think. I think, as we are all so tired (we went down in the morning to Piræeus, and have not walked less than thirty furlongs on a stretch), I think, it would not be unadvisable for us to sit down under the shade of these olives on the [*] inscribed pillar, and rest

[*] Joannes Matthias Gesnerus, who cannot for his life conceive how four men can sit upon a pillar, while it stands upright, proposes to alter the original ἐπιγεγραμμένης, which he neither will nor will not allow to mean *inscribed*, to ἀναδεδραμμένης *overturned*. A pillar, he believes, when it is thrown down, whether it have any inscription upon it or not, may be a very good thing to sit upon; but, while it stands upright, is fit for nothing but to be gazed at. But, supposing this pillar (pace tanti viri) to be lying all along, still retaining the letters with which it had been formerly inscribed, would a seat upon it for that reason be the less easy? and what should hinder any person acquainted with the convenience it afforded from recollecting the circumstance of its containing an inscription? Rather would not the contrary be

rest ourselves awhile out of the scorching of this meridian sun. When we are recovered a little from

be a strong proof of inattention? Or was the brain of Gesnerus intended to be only the repository of abstract ideas?

The mirror of such a critick is not sufficiently polished to reflect a perfect likeness; and he forgets, or never knew, that a description is a picture which fixes the attention by being complete in all its parts. Si tum est brevitas, cum tantum verborum est, quantum necesse est: aliquando id opus est, sed sæpe obest vel maxime in narrando, non solum quod obscuritatem affert, sed etiam quod eam virtutem, quæ narrationis est maxima, ut jucunda, et ad persuadendum accommodata sit, tollit. Videant illam.

" Nam is postquam excessit ex ephebis—
Quam longa est narratio! mores adolescentis ipsius, est servilis percunctatio, mors Chrysidis, vultus et forma, et lamentatio sororis, reliqua pervarie, jucundeque narrantur. Quod si hanc brevitatem quæsisset.

" Efferur, imus, ad sepulchrum venimus, in ignem posita" est decem versiculis totum conficere potuisset: quanquam hoc ipsum, " Efferur, imus," concisum est ita, ut non brevitati servitum sit, sed magis venustati. Quod si nihil fuisset, nisi " in ignem posita est," tamen res tota cognosci facile potuisset: sed et festivitatem habet narratio distinctis personis, et interpuncta sermonibus: et est probabilius, si, quod gestum esse dicas, quemadmodum actum sit, exponas: et multo apertius ad intelligendum est, si consistitur aliquandiu, ac non illa brevitate percurritur. Cicero de Oratore, 2.

from our fatigue, we can get up, you know, and make the best of our way to the city.

SAMIPPUS.

What, you fancy yourself still at Athens My good Sir, be pleased to recollect, that you are on a plain before the walls of Babylon, surrounded on all sides with an army, and attending a council of war.

> Beneath a church-yard yew,
> Decay'd and worn with age,
> At dusk of eve 'methought I spy'd
> Poor Slender's ghost, that whimpering cry'd,
> O sweet, O sweet Anne Page.
> Shenstone.

You may as well go about to turn the sun to ice by fanning in his face with a peacock's feather.
Shakespeare.

The rogues slighted me into the river with as little remorse, as they would have drowned a bitch's blind puppies, fifteen i' th' litter.
Shakespeare.

A sword, a better never did sustain itself upon a soldier's thigh. Shakespeare.

In these quotations, the yew being decayed and worn with age, the feather being a peacock's, the number and blindness of the puppies, and the soldier's thigh, are circumstances no otherwise necessary than as they serve to satisfy the imagination by compleating the picture.
See Elements of Criticism, vol. III. 174.

LYCINUS.

I beg your pardon. I had like to have forgot myself so far as to be in my right senses; notwithstanding my being otherwise engaged.

SAMIPPUS.

I am for advancing as soon as you please. I hope you will suffer no dangers to dismay you, nor discover any unwelcome proofs of your descent. The enemy is now upon us. The God of war is the word. The moment the trumpet sounds, do you set up a shout, and rush furiously on. Push your spears against the shields of the enemy, and keep them so closely engaged, as to give them no opportunity of galling us with their missive weapons. Now we come to close quarters. Timolaus, with the left wing, has repulsed the Medes. My troops bravely maintain their ground, though without gaining any advantage; for the Persians, encouraged by the presence of their king, fight desperately. The whole body of the Barbarian horse are charging our right wing. Now, Lycinus, is the time to distinguish yourself. Animate

mate your men by your example to sustain the shock.

LYCINUS.

Alas! poor me! all upon me! Could the Barbarian horse find nobody else but me to fall upon with such fury? I am really not ambitious of being so honourably distinguished, and I think I had best get out of their way, while I can. I have a good mind to run with all the speed I am able to the palæstra, and leave you in the heat of the battle, to shift for yourselves.

SAMIPPUS.

By no means. I insist on your having a share in the victory. For my part, I am to engage with the king in single combat. He challenges me, you see, and I cannot in honour refuse him.

LYCINUS.

Yes, truly, and you must not expect to come off without losing a little of your blood; which, in a royal contest, is no doubt a very fine thing.

SAMIPPUS.

You are right. I have received a flesh wound; but it is so slight, and is in such a part, that it will hardly be seen. I shall not have a disagreeable scar from it. Did you mind how I charged? I drove my lance through both him and his horse at once. I cut off his head, and took away his diadem from him; by which I am now become a king to all intents and purposes, being adored by all. But let Barbarians adore their king. I will be content to govern you as Greeks, under the title of commander in chief. Now only think with yourselves, what a number of cities I shall build, which I shall call by my name; and how many I shall take and destroy, if they should ever dare to mutter a word against me. Above all, now I have it in my power, I will be soundly revenged on my neighbour Cydias, who, notwithstanding his being so very rich, must needs invade my property, and drive me out of my farm.

LYCINUS.

Reſt yourſelf a little, Samippus. After obtaining ſo ſignal a victory, what do you ſay to feaſt at Babylon on the occaſion? But, I believe, your empire is gone by, and it is now Timolaus's turn to wiſh.

SAMIPPUS.

But what do you think of me, Lycinus? Have not I wiſhed like a prince?

LYCINUS.

Yes, moſt royal Sir, you have outdone Adimantus all to nothing. He indeed wallowed in luxury, and drank to his friends out of golden cups two talents [o] in weight; but he could not boaſt like you of being wounded in ſingle combat, nor had he your conſolation of never being free from fears and cares night and day. Neither was it your open enemies alone, from whom you had every thing to apprehend: but you found yourſelf expoſed to numberleſs ſe-

[o] One hundred and thirteen pounds, ten ounces, one penny-weight, ten grains and a half, troy weight.

cret and dangerous plots, you were envied, hated [*p*], flatttered. Not a single friend to confide in! every countenance entirely influenced by hope or fear! Even in a dream you could have no real satisfaction, nothing more than a mere vision of pomp, and purple, and gold, with a white fillet tied round your forehead, and your guards strutting before you. Your other enjoyments were intolerable fatigue and abundant disgust. Ambassadors must be attended to, justice administered, edicts issued forth. A nation perhaps has revolted; perhaps your kingdom is invaded. You fear this, suspect that. Possibly to others you may appear happy, but you never can think so yourself. This too is a very provoking circumstance, that you are liable to be sick, just like an ordinary man. A fever will pay you no respect, because you are a king; and death will laugh at lifeguards. He comes when he thinks fit; and, unawed by your diadem, drags you weep-

---

[*p*] Flattery, in the opinion of Cicero, and many others, is the most subtle poison, the most certain destroyer of human happiness. Sic habendum est, nullam in amicitia pestem esse majorem, quam adulationem. Cicero de Amicitia. Sola quippe adulatio nequicquam vigilantibus satellibus imperium depraedatur, regumque nobilissimam partem, animum nimirum, aggreditur. Synesius de Regno.

ing

ing away. Fallen from such a height, pulled down from your regal throne, you muſt tread in the ſame path, and be driven along on a level with the herd of mankind. It is true, you leave behind you a [*q*] lofty ſepulchre, a tall pillar, or a pyramid pompouſly [*r*] inſcribed, the poſthumous vaunt of pride, which is thus made to continue, when life and ſenſe are loſt. But after all that can be done, thoſe ſtatues and temples raiſed by adoring cities, together with the great man's mighty name, ſoon periſh, and are ſoon forgotten. And, indeed, were they to laſt ever ſo long, a dead man would hardly find himſelf much the better for them. The life of a king, you ſee, is a continued ſeries of labours, cares, and fears; and, when once your breath is gone, what are you better than any body elſe?—But it is your turn now, Timolaus; and I hope you will make a better uſe of the opportunity than your companions have done, by wiſhing like a man of ſenſe, who knows what he is about.

[*q*] It was uſual to raiſe a mount on a great man's grave.
Et regum cineres extructo monte quieſcunt.
Lucan. VIII.

[*r*] ιγγραμμον τας γωνιας, well inſcribed in the corners.

TI-

TIMOLAUS.

You will judge for yourself, Lycinus, if I be guilty of any impropriety, so as to subject myself to censure. As for gold, and treasures, and bushels of money, I care not for them. I am not, as you may suppose, so ridiculous as to wish for kingdoms or wars. I want not to be put in continual fear. I am not ignorant of the uncertainty of such possessions, which would expose me to so much mischief, and in which there is so much more of the bitter than the sweet. My wish is, that my good-natured Mercury would bestow on me a certain number of rings [1]. One, having the virtue in it to preserve my body invulnerable, not liable to any disease, always in full health and strength. Another, which, like that of Gyges, may conceal the wearer. Another, to give me the force of ten thousand men, to enable me singly to lift any weight with greater ease than they can do all together. Another, to give me the power of flying aloft in the air. Another, to

[1] The magical virtue of rings was in great estimation amongst the ancients.

lay afleep any perfon or perfons, whomfoever I pleafe; and to make every bolt and bar give way, and every door fly open at my approach. Laſt and beſt of all, let me have a moſt delightful ring to make me always lovely in every eye; that all manner of perfons, without any exception, may be fo fmitten with my charms, as to love me to diftraction, to be always longing for me, and to talk of me continually. I would have the men to go mad, and the women to hang themfelves in defpair. With a kind look let me confer happinefs, let my neglect enfure perdition. In fhort, let me go far beyond whatever has been related of Hyacinthus, of Hylas, or Phaon. All thefe privileges I would enjoy, not merely for the fhort fpace ufually allotted to the life of man. I wifh to live a thoufand years, but my youth never to exceed feventeen, ftripping off old age as a fnake does his fkin. Having thofe advantages, I could never be in want of any thing. For, as I can open all doors, lay afleep all guards, and enter any where unfeen, whatever belongs to others I can eafily make my own. If there fhould be any fine fight, any valuable

poffeffion,

poffeffion, any thing good to eat or drink, in
the Indies, or at the Pole, I fhpuld not wait
till it was brought to me, but would fly in-
ftantly to it, and indulge to my heart's content.
I fhould take an opportunity of feeing the
Griffin, that winged beaft; and that Indian
bird, equally rare, the Phœnix, which nobody
elfe ever faw. I fhould difcover the head of
the Nile, which has never been done before,
and vifit all the uninhabited parts of this earth;
not forgetting the Antipodes of the other he-
mifphere, if any fuch people there are. As
for the ftars, and the moon, and even the fun,
I could very eafily fcrape acquaintance with
them, as the heat would have no effect upon
me. What would be a very agreeable thing,
I fhould be able to tell the news of an Olympick victory at Babylon, on the very day it
was obtained; and, though I had dined in Syria, I might fup in Italy. If I had a mind to
be fecretly revenged on an enemy, I fhould
have nothing to do but to let fall a great ftone,
and beat out his brains, while nobody would
know any thing of the matter. I fhould have
an equal opportunity of ferving my friends, for

I could

I could pour them down plenty of gold, as they lay asleep. If I should chance to meet with a proud, tyrannical, rich, saucy fellow, I would take him up with me into the air about twenty furlongs, and dash him down headlong. As I could enter invisibly into any chamber and lay every body fast asleep, except those I wished to be awake, I should meet with no interruption in my amours. What do you say to be out of harm's way, up in the air, beholding enemies engaged in battle? If I should take it into my head, you know, I might join those who had the worst of it, rally them as they were running away, and give them the victory, subduing their conquerors by sleep. Upon the whole, I would make human life my sport, being master of whatever the world could bestow, nothing less than a God in the eyes of other men. Thus enjoying the most perfect health through the whole course of so long a life, I shall be sensible of the highest felicity, which can neither be destroyed nor endangered. And now, Lycinus, what unfavourable reflections have you to make?

LY-

LYCINUS.

None at all. You do not suppose, that I would set my wit against a man with wings, and with more strength than ten thousand. I shall only beg leave to ask a question. In the many nations over which you have flown, did you never see another * old fellow, mounted also on a little ring, and equally unsettled in his mind, with a bald head, and a flat nose, beloved by all manner of persons, and able to remove mountains with his little finger? Will you also resolve me this? why cannot one ring answer all your purposes, but you must be encumbered with so many, that every finger of your left hand is insufficient, and you are obliged to have recourse to your right; When, after all that has been said and done, you still want one the most necessary of all: I mean, to keep your nose clean, and clear your head. Or, will a good substantial draught of hellebore do it?

TIMOLAUS.

But come, Lycinus, let us hear your wise wish. You, who find so much fault with other people, will, no doubt, take good care to be unblamable yourself.

* Meaning perhaps Saturn, or Time.

LYCINUS.

I have no occasion to give myself any trouble about it, for we are just at Dipylon. Our good friend Samippus, with his duel at Babylon; and you, Timolaus, who dine in Syria and sup in Italy, have engrossed the whole way with your own wishes, leaving me none for mine. Which, to tell you the truth, I am not at all sorry for; as I shall not, like you, after a slight glimpse of transitory riches, as little real as an addled egg, feel the cutting mortification of being again reduced to my homely fare. You wake from your delectable dream, when, behold! your treasures, your diadems, your riches, your happiness, have taken wing and are gone! No other enjoyment is then found to reside within your walls besides the miserable meal of poverty. You will then change your tone, and be willing to confess, that you have been only actors, not a whit superior to those mighty personages, the Creons, or Agamemnons, who, "having strutted their hour upon the stage," retire supperless to bed, and then "are heard no more." You, Timolaus,

laus, may be considered as another Icarus, who must lose not only your wings but your rings too, and be contented to tread the ground. It is enough for me, as I cannot conveniently take Babylon, nor be the master of so much wealth, to have the pleasure of laughing at your ridiculous wishes, which have not been, I think, in every respect becoming such great philosophers.

THE FUGITIVES.

APOLLO, JUPITER, PHILOSOPHY, HERCULES, MERCURY, MEN, MASTER, ORPHEUS, FUGITIVE, DEFENDANT.

APOLLO.

IS it true, father, that an old man, having a propensity to excite admiration, threw himself into the fire, in presence of the many thousands assembled at the Olympick Games?

We have been told so by the moon, who says, she actually saw him burning.

JUPITER.

It is too true, Apollo. I wish it were otherwise.

APOLLO.

What, he was a very worthy man, I suppose, too good to be burnt?

JUPITER.

I say nothing to that; but this I can say, for I have not forgot, that I was almost poisoned with the smoke. You cannot be at a loss to imagine what kind of fume proceeds from the body of a roasting man. I do assure you, that, if I had not got away, as fast as I could, into Arabia, I could not possibly have survived it. Even after I was there, surrounded with so many sweets, such rich aromaticks, such abundance of incense, my nostrils hardly ceased still to retain that plaguy stench. I am almost ready to spew at the thoughts of it.

APOLLO.

APOLLO.

Pray, Jupiter, what could he mean? What good can it do a man to leap into a fire, and be burnt to a cinder?

JUPITER.

Nay, my child, if you talk in this manner, you would censure Empedocles, who did so before him. Empedocles, you know, jumped down the chimney of Mount Ætna.

APOLLO.

Poor man! I am sorry he was so much out of his senses. But what could be the occasion of this man's conceiving such an unaccountable whim?

JUPITER.

For that matter he made a publick apology for choosing his manner of dying, which I will repeat to you as well as I can remember. He said — But what female is that, who advances towards us with such hasty steps? She sheds tears, and appears to be full of trouble. It must be Philosophy, and no other, that calls upon me with so piteous a tone. What is the matter? What makes you weep so, my daughter? How came you to leave the world? Have the fools formed a conspiracy against you, and would they destroy you too, as Anytus did Socrates? Is it for that you have taken your flight?

PHILOSOPHY.

No such thing, father. Those good people, the mob, have always been loud in my praises. They reverenced, honoured, admired, and did every thing but adore me. To be sure, they did not much understand what I said; but no matter for that. It was—I do not know what I am to call them—my acquaintance, my friends, I suppose, I must say, since they call themselves by my name—they are the persons, by whom I have been most grievously abused.

JUPITER.

Philosophers in a plot against Philosophy! do you say?

PHI.

PHILOSOPHY.

No, Sir, not Philosophers. Philosophers and Philosophy have equal cause to complain.

JUPITER.

Who is it then that has injured you? Since neither fools, nor Philosophers, have offended you, who is it?

PHILOSOPHY.

There are certain persons, Jupiter, who are neither the one nor the other, but between both. In dress, in mien, in gait, in manner, they resemble me. But these several circumstances are at variance with their other half, their vulgar half. They enroll themselves under my name, as if intending to follow my standard. They call themselves my disciples, my familiar friends and companions. Meanwhile their manner of life is altogether unseemly, altogether unsuitable to such a pretence, being nothing better than a tissue of ignorance, impudence, and wantonness. All this, father, is no small disgrace to philosophy, and, in short,

short, is such treatment as I could no longer endure. I have therefore shewn them a light pair of heels, and am come hither to complain.

JUPITER.

You had very good reason. But pray what was your principal grievance?

PHILOSOPHY.

No trifle, believe me. You know, father, when you beheld the world filled with iniquity and injustice, a mere jumble of ignorance and ill-manners, in pure compassion to misguided mortals, you sent me down amongst them, giving me a strict charge, that I should insist on their behaving better for the future. I was to prevail with them, if possible, to lay aside their brutality, to abstain from acts of violence, and to forbear injuring one another. And that they might establish a more peaceable mode of life, I was directed to call their attention to the truth. What passed on my receiving my commission is still fresh in my memory: " You see, daughter, said you, the effect of the ignorance which prevails. Mens' manners

are

are universally corrupted. I pity their blindness, and have resolved on dispatching you amongst them, as being the only one of us I can think of, who is competent to the cure of their folly, and likely to put an end to the madness of the present proceedings."

JUPITER.

I remember I said a good deal to that purpose. But pray tell me what kind of reception you met with at your first flying down, and how they treat you at present. I desire to know.

PHILOSOPHY.

I was not in so great a hurry to go to the Greeks. As I conceived it to be a work of greater difficulty, I thought it best to begin with the instruction of Barbarians. The Greeks I left to themselves for the present, having no manner of doubt of easily bringing them to my mind at any time, and reducing to rule a people already so well prepared to receive my laws [*t*]. I made the best of my way to India.

[*t*] A true account of the progress of philosophy. Solanus.

The

The Indians, the greatest nation in the universe, were without any considerable difficulty prevailed upon to alight from their elephants, and listen to me. The [u] Bramins, that happy race of men living on the confines of the Nechræi and Oxydracæ, are entirely at my disposal. Their lives are regulated by my precepts, and they are of course greatly respected by all their neighbours. There is something to excite your admiration in their manner of dying.

JUPITER.

You are speaking of the Gymnosophists. I have heard much of them. They get upon

[u] The Brachmanes are described by ancient historians, as a nation of philosophers, who eat no flesh, and drank no wine. As heat and cold were to them equally indifferent, they wore no clothes, whence they had the name of Gymnosophists, or the naked philosophers. It is very remarkable, that these Indian sages continue almost the same as their ancestors to this very day, being perhaps the only people of the world, in whose customs, manners, and opinions, some thousands of years have produced hardly any alteration. A great deal might be added on this curious subject. Compare Pliny, Quintus Curtius, Strabo, Arrian, Cicero's Tusc. quæst. 5. &c. with the several late accounts of Hindostan, by Scrafton, Holwell, Dow, and others.

the

the top of a vaft funeral pile, and fuffer themfelves to be burnt to afhes with the greateft compofure imaginable, never once fhifting, or flinching, or changing countenance. Though perhaps this is no fuch mighty matter, as I have lately feen fomething of the fame kind at the Olympick games. You were there, I fuppofe, at the burning of the old man?

PHILOSOPHY.

No; I was afraid to go thither, on account of thofe mifcreants, which I have juft told you of. I faw them repairing to Olympia in great numbers, that they might have an opportunity of amufing themfelves with abufing the company, and make the [x] back part of the temple ring with their noife. It was owing to this cir-

[x] Οπισθοδομ- was that part of the temple oppofed to προναος, where common criers, philofophers, and other talkers, were ufed to addrefs the publick. Joannes Matthias Gefnerus, in the moft friendly manner, advifes us not to miftake this part of the Temple of Jupiter Olympius for that belonging to the Temple of Minerva, at Athens. Which is the very fame thing, and juft as neceffary, as to tell a man in York minfter, that he is not in St. Paul's Cathedral, at London.

cumftance,

cumstance, that I did not see what you mention.—After leaving the Bramins, I immediately went down into [y] Æthiopia, and from thence into Ægypt, where I conversed with the priests and prophets; to whom having communicated my divine precepts, I went on to Babylon, in order to initiate the Chaldees and Magi. Then I proceeded to Scythia, and from thence into Thrace, where I was joined by Eumolpus and Orpheus, both which I sent before me into Greece; the former to perfect them in the divine mysteries (as he was well qualified for it by my instructions), and the latter to animate and confirm them in their sentiments by the force of his song. I myself immediately followed. On my first arrival amongst them, the Greeks neither shewed any great signs of fondness, nor did they absolutely reject me. However, after some degree of intimacy amongst them, I met with a small number, who were not unwilling to be considered as my disciples. They were, it must be owned, a very small number. I had one from Samos, one from

[y] Solanus observes upon this passage, that he never heard of any Æthiopian philosophers.

Ephesus,

Ephesus, and one from Abdera. Not to be more particular, they were in all [z] seven. After those I do not know how it happened, that a tribe of [a] Sophists became my attendants, not thoroughly relishing my institutions, though they found reason to love them well

[z] The seven wise men of Greece, as they are called, were Pittacus, Bias, Thales, Periander, Cleobulus, Chilon, Solon. The following apophthegms, amongst others, still remain to evidence their wisdom:

Γνῶθι σεαυτόν. Know thyself. Solon.
Τέλος ὅρα μακρου βίου. Look to the end of a long life.
           Chilon.

Καιρὸν γνῶθι. Know the opportunity.
           Pittacus.

Οἱ πλειους κακοι. The majority are bad.
           Bias.

Μελέτη τὸ πᾶν. Every thing yields to industry.
           Periander.

Ἄριστον μέτρον. Moderation is best.
           Cleobulus.

Ἐγγύα, πάρα δ' ἄτη. Be a bondsman, ruin is ready.
           Thales.

[a] Τες σοφίας τὴν ἀργυρίου τῷ βουλομένῳ πωλοῦντας σοφιστὰς ἀποκαλοῦσι. They are called Sophists, who sell their wisdom for money to any body that wants such a thing. Xen. Mem. Soc. 1. 6. 13. Modern Sophs are happily free from this imputation, unless when they sell their books.

enough not to leave me. They bore some resemblance to the Centaur, as being neither one thing nor another, a kind of quagmire composition, made up of vanity and philosophy mixed up together, not altogether devoted to ignorance, but wanting sufficient resolution to fix their eyes steadily on truth. Like purblind persons, they were just able to perceive an obscure kind of image, an uncertain shadow of what they could not well make out; though with this difference, that, in their own opinion, they saw every thing very plainly. Hence their knowledge so useless, so superfluous, so minute, so irrefragable, as they fondly conceited! Hence those inexplicable labyrinths of words, those refined questions, those trim replies, produced by doubt, and ending in ignorance! As they could not but meet with repulses and reproofs from those who were really my friends, they must needs put themselves into a violent passion, and fall out with them. Till at last they had recourse to law, and sought redress in a draught of hemlock. As such worshipful society was no longer to be endured, it now became necessary for me to provide

for

for my safety by immediate flight. But Antisthenes and Diogenes, and afterwards Crates and Menippus, prevailed on me to defer my departure a little longer. Which I am sorry for; for, if I had gone off at once, I should not have been so great a sufferer.

JUPITER.

Hitherto you only give me to understand, that you are very much out of humour; but I do not know why.

PHILOSOPHY.

I will tell you, Jupiter. A mean servile set of wretches, many of them trained to a variety of low occupations, such as cobbling, hammering, fulling of cloth, preparing wool for the women to spin—all these, merely from the want of leisure, not to mention other reasons, must have found it impossible to cultivate any acquaintance with me, or even so much as to know my name. Notwithstanding which, when they were grown up to men, and consequently as wise as wise could be, they could not fail to observe the share which my associates had in the publick applause. People in general, they saw, willingly refigned themfelves to their authority, followed their advice, and ſtood in awe of their reprehenſions, patiently enduring whatever they were pleaſed to ſay, and thinking it no mean thing to be the ſubjects of their converſation. Such advantages as theſe were not to be neglected. Although at the ſame time it was found, that to learn the ſeveral requiſites for this way of life, would be at leaſt very tedious and tireſome, if not utterly impoſſible. Trades, however, as they knew by experience, were ſlippery and uncertain, very laborious, yet hardly affording a ſufficiency. Servitude was to ſome of them a burden too heavy to be borne. They reſolved therefore on venturing all in one bold puſh. Being ſteadily attached to their own fond conceits, they brought over to their party audaciouſneſs, ignorance, and impudence, hopeful allies, on whoſe countenance and ſupport they might always depend. They next invented new terms of reproach, and ribaldry, to be always ready at the tongue's end, amply ſufficient to diſtinguiſh their profeſſion. You ſee, Jupiter, how apt the equipage is to the expedition! In their outward

appear-

appearance they are certainly very paſſable. With
ſuch a form and garb they are not farther diftant from Philoſophy than Æſop's aſs was unlike
a lion. And, you know, he met with ſeveral
perſons not at leiſure to diſallow his pretenſions. As to what lies open to the eye, you
need not be told, that it is no matter of difficulty to mimick an appearance. It is eaſy
enough to wrap up one's ſhoulders in a cloak,
or to hang a wallet over one's back. To carry
a great ſtick in one's hand, to make a noiſe like
the barking of a dog, or the braying of an
aſs, and to abuſe every body one meets, are
ſuch accompliſhments as a man of ordinary talents needs not deſpair of attaining. Beſides,
ſuch is the reverence paid to the habit, that
they found themſelves perfectly ſecure, and
under no apprehenſions of a ſuitable return for
their inſolence. Liberty to them becomes a
thing of courſe, however much againſt the in-
clinations of their maſter; who, were he dif-
poſed to aſſert his claim to their ſervitude,
might be pretty certain of a ſalute from their
ſtaves. They no longer put up with their former allowance of pulſe, thyme, or ſalt fiſh;
but are in a condition to gratify themſelves
with

with the best of every thing, and in the greatest
plenty. They fill their bellies with variety of
dainties, and drink the richest wines. As for
money, they may make themselves easy about
that; having nothing more to do than to gather in their tributes, or, as they express it
themselves, to shear their sheep at their leisure;
being always confident of a general good reception, either from a reverence for their profession, or a fear of their abuse. Since nobody
troubles his head with looking any farther than
to the mere outside, they think they have dif-
covered, that a real philosopher is on no better
footing than themselves. Indeed they are not
fond of being asked any questions, though
ever so civilly. On the slightest interrogatory,
they directly roar out, fly to their fort, display
their bad language, and brandish their stick.
If you ask for deeds, they give you words.
If you are disposed to examine the latter, they
bid you look at the former. Thus the whole
city is become a scene of iniquity, chiefly by
means of the followers of Diogenes, Antisthenes, and the surly Crates. These Cynicks are
careful to avoid whatever is laudable in the
conduct of their namesake. The watchfulness,

the

the fidelity, the attention to his mafter, the memory of the dog they leave to the emulation of others. Their labour is to excel him in whatever qualities he has that refemble their own. They bark, they lick their lips, they fwallow, they rend, they fnap, they tear, they intrigue, they coax, they fawn, they flatter; meanwhile, whoever gives a dinner, or any thing good, may depend on their company. The confequence of all this will be, that, in a fhort time, you will fee every mechanick quit his fhop, and leave his trade to take care of itfelf; as he finds by experience, that his utmoft labour and diligence, his conftant employment early and late, will hardly procure him common neceffaries; while he beholds a fet of lazy impoftors wallowing in abundance, impofing taxes like tyrants, and raifing them as readily, enraged when they happen not to fucceed, and not contented when they do. They may very well think it a golden age: they need but open their mouths to have them filled with honey. However, this is not all the mischief they do. For, though they are, it muft be owned, as to their outward appearance moft grave and venerable, the difgrace they bring

upon me by their libidinous manners, is better
concealed in silence. I shall only observe, that
they are as fond of making proselytes of the
wives of their friends, as ever Paris was. The
fair philosophers being thus reconciled, as they
pretend, to the institutes of [b] Plato, are made
common to all; though one may very fairly
suppose them ignorant of what Plato really intended, and that his divine precepts do not at
all accord with their practices. To talk of
their behaviour at feasts, and in their cups,
would take up too much time. While they
rail so loudly against intemperance, wantonness,
avarice, and unlawful love, they are themselves
most notoriously in the commission of every
act they condemn. For no two things in nature can vary more than what they say and
what they do. As for example, flattery is what
they would make you believe they have an
aversion to, though in the practice of that art
no Gnathonides or Strouthias, was ever found
to equal them. Truth is what they recommend to others; but, as for themselves, they
cannot open their mouths without uttering a
lie. Epicurus is a declared enemy; pleasure

[b] Plato's Republick, Dialogue the fifth.

they pretend to abhor, though in reality it is the secret spring which moves all their actions. They are gentlemen very easily put out of humour. A young child will not sooner be induced to make a noise about nothing. It occasions often no little pleasantry to see their choler rising and boiling over with the least trifle. Their cheeks are immediately transformed to the complection of lead. Their eyes appear wild and distracted; while their mouths are filled with rage, and distil poison. I wish you were only to be a witness of the stuff that falls from their tongues. " As for such things as gold or silver, they say, far be it from us to covet the possession. An obolus, to purchase our pulse, suffices us. And the fountain, or the river, affords us such liquor as we are contented with." But scarcely are these fine speeches out of their mouths, than they fall to work in every way imaginable, not to earn an obolus, or a drachma, but to rake together as much as they can possibly get. Philosophy brings home a freight more profitable than that of the merchant. And accordingly, when they think they have got enough, and laid in a sufficient stock of supplies, they throw away their difmal old cloak, and buy themſelves fashionable clothes. After purchafing eftates, and monopolifing whole neighbourhoods, with a train of fpruce attendants, they bid a final adieu to the wallet of Crates, the tattered robe of Antifthenes, and the tub of Diogenes. People in general, feeing thefe pretty doings, will of courfe ceafe having to do with philofophers; for, as they think them all alike, every thing amifs is laid to my charge. By which means it has been for a confiderable time impoffible to prevail with any one individual of them to come over to my party. And in fhort, my work goes on like [c] Penelope's web,

[c] Penelope's hufband Ulyſſes was abfent from her twenty years, during all which time her conjugal fidelity fuffered not the leaft diminution, notwithftanding her numerous fuitors, fome of which were fo very prefling, that fhe found it neceffary to filence their importunities by promifing compliance as foon as fhe had finifhed a web which fhe had in hand; to delay the finifhing of which as long as poffible, or till her hufband's return, it was her conftant cuftom to undo by night what fhe had done by day. Let no impertinent wit here recollect, that, when at laft her hufband did come, his loving fpoufe did not fo much as know him; nor was he remembered by any one of the family excepting only a poor old

web, no sooner done than undone. All the pains I can take, every thing I can do, being thus rendered

old dog, who juſt lived to expreſs his joy at his maſter's return, and inſtantly died. See Hom. Od. II. and XVII.

Thus, near the gates conferring as they drew,
Argus, the dog, his ancient maſter knew;
He, not unconſcious of the voice, and tread,
Lifts to the ſound his ear, and rears his head;
Bred by Ulyſſes, nouriſh'd at his board,
But ah! not fated long to pleaſe his lord!
To him, his ſwiftneſs and his ſtrength were vain;
The voice of glory call'd him o'er the main,
Till then in every ſilvan chaſe renown'd,
With Argus, Argus, rang the woods around;
With him the youth purſu'd the goat or fawn,
Or trac'd the mazy leveret o'er the lawn.
Now left to man's ingratitude he lay,
Unhous'd, neglected in the publick way.
And where on heaps the rich manure was ſpread,
Obſcene with reptiles, took his ſordid bed.

He knew his lord; he knew, and ſtrove to meet;
In vain he ſtrove to crawl, and kiſs his feet;
Yet (all he could) his tail, his ears, his eyes
Salute his maſter, and confeſs his joys.
Soft pity touch'd the mighty maſter's ſoul,
Adown his cheek a tear unbidden ſtole;
Stole unperceiv'd; he turn'd his head and dry'd
The drop humane: then thus impaſſion'd cry'd;
What noble beaſt in this abandon'd ſtate
Lies here all helpleſs at Ulyſſes' gate?

His

dered of no avail, ignorance and wickedness look on and laugh at me.

J U.

His bulk and beauty speak no vulgar praise;
If, as be seems, he was in better days,
Some care his age deserves: or was he priz'd
For worthless beauty! therefore now despis'd?
Such dogs, and men there are, mere things of state,
And always cherish'd by their friends, the great.

Not Argus so, (Eumæus thus rejoin'd)
But serv'd a master of a nobler kind,
Who never, never shall behold him more!
Long, long since perish'd on a distant shore!
Oh had you seen him, vigorous, bold, and young,
Swift as a stag, and as a lion strong;
Him no fell savage on the plain withstood,
None 'scap'd him, bosom'd in the gloomy wood;
His eye how piercing, and his scent how true,
To wind the vapour in the tainted dew!
Such, when Ulysses left his natal coast;
Now years unnerve him, and his lord is lost!
The women keep the generous creature bare,
A sleek and idle race is all their care:
The master gone, the servants what restrains?
Or dwells humanity where riot reigns?
Jove fix'd it certain, that whatever day
Makes man a slave, takes half his worth away.

This said, the honest herdsman strode before:
The musing monarch pauses at the door;

The

JUPITER.

O ye Gods! what evils has philosophy been made to endure! How grievously have those villains offended! It is high time for us to resolve on some method of punishment. The thunder-bolt makes quick work. It kills at a blow.

APOLLO.

Give me leave, father, to speak. I hate the rascals as much as you can do. In behalf of the muses, I disdain whatever is so averse from their influence. But I cannot think such paltry offenders worthy the honour of provoking a thun-

---

<small>The dog whom fate had granted to behold
His lord, when twenty tedious years had roll'd,
Takes a last look, and, having seen him, dies;
So clos'd for ever faithful Argus' eyes!
           Pope's Translation.

This episode, than which nothing can be more beautiful or affecting, has been ridiculed by Perrault and others, "mere things of slate," who never "dry'd the drop humane."</small>

derbolt, or perishing by the arm of Jove. If you think fit, I could wish that Mercury might be deputed to assign them their punishment. As he is a good scholar, so he will be able to judge of their several pretensions; and able to distinguish who is really a philosopher, and who is not. To those truly meriting that appellation, he will not refuse their share of praise; and he will punish others, as occasion may require.

JUPITER.

I am very much obliged to you, Apollo, for your hint. I am of opinion, that Hercules too, taking Philosophy with him, should go down immediately to earth. If you can but extirpate those monsters, Hercules, you may set it down as a thirteenth labour not inferior to any of the twelve.

HERCULES.

Sooner than have any thing to do with them, I had much rather undertake to cleanse another Augæan stable. But, if we must go, we must go.

PHILOSOPHY.

Our father's good pleasure muſt determine ours; though, I own, I ſhall go very much againſt my will.

MERCURY.

Let us go directly. We may do the buſineſs of ſome of them this very day. We muſt aſk you, Philoſophy, where they are to be found. Though, I take it for granted, Greece is the country.

PHILOSOPHY.

Indeed, Mercury, you are very much miſtaken. There are a few, a very few philoſophers in Greece, and thoſe few are really and truly what their name denotes. But the philoſophers, who are the object of our commiſſion, have no appetite for the homely fare of Attica. What they aim at is plenty of ſilver and gold, and our ſearch is to be directed accordingly.

MER-

MERCURY.

Suppose then we make the best of our way to Thrace?

HERCULES.

With all my heart: I will shew you the way; I have been there so often, that I am very well acquainted with the country. This is the way!

MERCURY.

Which?

HERCULES.

Do not you see, both of you, yonder two mountains, the two greatest and most beautiful of all others? Hæmus is the larger of the two, and over against it is Rhodope. From each side below are extended very fertile plains. There are three or four beautiful summits, gradually rising like the spires of an approaching city. And behold! yonder is the city!

MER-

MERCURY.

Yes verily, Hercules, the most large and beautiful city ever seen. Its splendour is very conspicuous at this distance, and it seems to be washed by a very large river.

HERCULES.

Yes, the Hebrus. The [d] city was built by Philip. We are now below the clouds, very near to the earth. So we may land, if you please. Success to us!

MERCURY.

With all my heart. But what is to be done now? How shall we trace them out?

HERCULES.

That, Mercury, depends upon you. You can easily cry them: it is your trade, you know.

[d] Philippolis, anciently called Poneropolis; and, in Pliny's time, Trimontium.

MERCURY.

The only difficulty is in not knowing their names. Philosophy, I hope, will be so good as to describe them, and tell me besides what I am to call them.

PHILOSOPHY.

I cannot tell you for certain what names they go by, not being so much acquainted with them. But, from the very great desire which they have to be rich, I think you might venture to call them by [*e*] some name expressive of that passion.

MERCURY.

Very right. But who are those persons coming up to us? What can they be in quest of? They are going to enquire of us concerning something or other.

MEN.

Pray, gentlemen, can you inform us—or can you, madam, give us any account of three

---

[*e*] Several such names are proposed in the original.

impostors, which you may have chanced to observe together. Or, have you seen a masculine, man-looking woman, close shaved in the [g] Spartan mode?

PHILOSOPHY.

So! they are engaged in the same pursuit with ourselves.

MEN.

You mistake. It cannot be. The persons we seek are fugitives. And amongst them is a female, which they haye spirited away.

MERCURY.

You shall judge of the reasons of our search. Let us immediately cry them. Whoever can give information of a Paphlagonian slave, a Barbarian from Sinope, having his name from his love of money, his complexion somewhat of the palest, with a smooth skin, and a long beard, carrying a wallet and wearing a cloak, easily provoked to anger, illiterate, a stranger

[g] It was the fashion, it seems, for the Spartan Virgins to be shaved immediately before their marriage. The hair was consecrated to some friendly deity.

to all that is elegant, with a rough voice, and full of abuse—whoever will make discovery of such a person [*b*] may do it on his own terms.

MASTER.

I believe, Sir, I can pretty well guess who it is you mean. My man Beetle was such a person as you describe. He cherished his beard, and, being no stranger to my trade, understood very well how to crop his hair. I am a fuller, and he was used to sit in my shop, and [*i*] smooth away the superfluities from the cloth.

PHILOSOPHY.

He was your servant; but of late his art of a fuller has been exercised upon himself; for he is now trimmed up in the shape of a philosopher.

[*b*] " Such a person may have his wine" is the translation of Spence and others. They know best what they mean.

[*i*] Regrating from re, again, and the French gratter, to grate, or scrape, signifieth the scraping or dressing of cloth, or other goods, in order for selling the same again.

Burn's Justice.

So that this pretended philosopher was neither more nor less than a Regrater.

MASTER.

MASTER.

Beetle a philosopher! and no longer to pay any attention to me! what astonishing assurance!

MEN.

We shall find them all, I do not question. Philosophy knows very well what she is about.

PHILOSOPHY.

But who is he that comes now? Pray, friend Hercules, who is this fine fellow with the [k] harp?

HERCULES.

That is Orpheus. He sailed with me to Argos. He sings an excellent song. Nobody can be dull where he is. We were so cheered

---

[k] O την κιθαραν] Subaudi * εχων.

Franciscus Gujetus.

* O Gujete! Credatne quis te Lucianum perlegisse. Perlegisti tamen, et probasti alibi ellipsin, nec meministi perpetuo εχων in hisce omitti.
Joannes Fredericus Reitzius.

Alas! Grjetus, that thy memory should here fail thee, and expose thee to the pity of Joannes Fredericus Reitzius!

with

with his strains, that we rowed on lustily, and never dreamed of being tired. Hail, Orpheus, thou best, thou most musical of mankind! I hope you have not forgot Hercules.

ORPHEUS.

Certainly not. I know you well, all three of you; Philosophy, Hercules, and Mercury. But am not I to have the reward, being so well acquainted with the person you enquire after?

MERCURY.

The son of Calliope must be a great deal too wise to want any money; and, I dare say, will tell us where he is without more ado.

ORPHEUS.

You are very much in the right, to be sure. I can point out to you the house where he lives. But as to shewing you the man himself, I had rather be excused. He is a very foul-mouthed fellow; his only study is abuse, and I want none of it.

MERCURY.

Well, only shew us the house.

OR-

ORPHEUS.

It is the very next door. But I do not wish for a sight of him, and will take myself away.

MERCURY.

Hark! do not I hear somebody with a female voice reciting Homer?

PHILOSOPHY.

It is even so. Let us listen.

FUGITIVE.

[*l*] Who lies and says, he loves not gold full well,
My soul abhors him as the gates of hell.

MERCURY.

Then I am sure your soul must abhor Beetle.
[*m*] Who treated ill his all-confiding friend.

[*l*] A Parody on Hom. Il. ix. 3 2. and Od. xix. 156.
[*m*] Hom. Il. iii. 354.

FRIEND.

Meaning me. I had entertained him in my house, and, in return for my hospitality, he very obligingly ran away with my wife.

FUGITIVE.

[n] A sot, with eyes of dog, and heart of deer.
  Unfit in arms or council to appear;
  Abusive brawler, chattering as a daw,
  Careless of who is king, or what is law!

MASTER.

How very pat!

FUGITIVE.

[o] A dog, a lion, and a goat between,
  Odorous as is the wildest scent obscene.

FRIEND.

What a sufferer you have been, madam, amongst so many sad dogs!—They say, Mercury, she is in a way to increase the number of them.

[n] Hom. Il. i. 225. and ii. 202, 214. 246.
[o] Hom. Il. vi. 181. Hesiod. Theog. 323.

MERCURY.

Never mind. Should she produce you a Cerberus, or a Geryon, Hercules, you know, may have some new employment.—But here they come. There is no occasion to knock at the door.

MASTER.

I have you now, Mr. Beetle. Hush! no words! Let us examine the contents of your wallet. I will see what you have got: Lupines, I suppose; or, perhaps, a crust of bread.

MERCURY.

Take my word for it, you will find yourself greatly mistaken. What do you say to a purse of gold?

HERCULES.

Wonder at nothing. In Greece he might pass for a Cynick; but here in good troth he is more of the cast of [*p*] Chrysippus. You

---

[*p*] A pun on the word Chrysippus, derived from χρυσος, gold; and ιππος, a horse.

will see him [*q*] Cleanthes in a little time. The mean rascal will hang himself by the hairs of his beard.

MASTER.

Hark you, you Sir, are not you my runaway, Greasy? The very same, I protest! What will this world come to? Greasy a philosopher! hah, hah, hah!

MERCURY.

There is a third man for you without a master.

MASTER.

I beg your pardon, Mercury. I am his master; and, by virtue of my authority, I give him liberty to go hang himself.

MERCURY.

What do you mean by that?

[*q*] Jacobus Palmerius a Grentemesnil, who can find no joke in Cleanthes, supposes, that Lucian might write Χρεμης, Chremes, which agrees so well with κρεμασθαι, will hang himself. Cleanthes, it seems, died of hunger; so had no occasion to hang himself.

MASTER.

Mean! Why, Sir, he is so very fragrant, we used to call him the perfume-pot.

MERCURY.

O Hercules, Hercules! thou averter of evil! What do I hear and see? A staff and a wallet! I pray you, good Sir, to take your wife.

FRIEND.

Not I. Would you have me take her back big with an old book?

MERCURY.

A book? [r] I do not understand you.

FRIEND.

A book, I tell you; a book with three heads.

[r] Nor I neither.

MER-

MERCURY.

Oh! mighty well! [s] Triphales too is comical.

[t] FUGITIVES.

Of what remains, Mercury, you are the proper judge.

MERCURY.

I am of opinion then, that this good lady, in order to avoid bringing a m ny-headed monster into the world, do instantly return to her husband in Greece. As for the two dirty fugitives, let them be delivered up to their masters, that they may lose no time in resuming their former occupations. Let one of them be employed in washing foul linen, and the other in mending old clothes. Only, first of all, let his

---

[s] Triphales was a play of Aristophanes, of which some fragments remain. But the wit of this allusion has slipped through the fingers of the Scholiasts. Of what species of joke it was may occur to the Reader, who has seen the words φαλλος and φαλλος.

[t] Moses du Soul thinks, this word Fugitives should give up its place to Hercules.

hide be well fuppled with a ftalk of [*u*] mal-
lows. Let this learned philofopher be fhaved
with a plaifter of ftinking pitch. Then let
my gentleman be conducted naked to Mount
Hæmus, there to remain in the fnow, with his
feet tied together.

FUGITIVES.

Alas! alas! dear me! what will become
of us!

MASTER.

Come, come, none of your tragedy-faces
here! Away with you, get you gone to thofe
who will fmooth your furface for you! Quick,
quick, off with your lion's fkin, that you may
be known for an afs as you are.

[*u*] Diofcorides and Mr. Miller mention the ufe of mallow
in foftening the belly, but fay nothing of its virtue, when
externally applied, in fuppling the back.

The [y] KINGFISHER; a Dialogue on Transformation.

CHÆREPHON and SOCRATES.

CHÆREPHON.

WHAT voice was that, Socrates, which we heard at a distance on the coast, so sweetly echoed from the promontory? What can it be? The inhabitants of the water are dumb: it could not be any one of them that utters sounds so pleasant to the ear.

SOCRATES.

It is a sea-bird, called the Kingfisher, concerning which there goes an [z] old story. .
It

---

[y] The commentators will not allow this to be a dialogue of Lucian, some of them thinking it too good, others too bad, to be of his writing. It has been attributed to Plato, and to one Leo, an Academick.

[z] Alcyone was the wife of Ceyx, king of Trachin, who being obstinately resolved on consulting the oracle of Apollo Clarius, concerning the state of his kingdom, was shipwrecked
in

It is continually crying and lamenting. This bird, they tell you, was formerly a woman, the daughter of Æolus, son of Hellen; and that she was married to a young man named Ceyx, a Trachinian, son of Lucifer, the morning star, the [a] handsome son of a handsome father. Some divine power having furnished her with wings, she flies over the sea, in search of her lost husband, having in vain explored every land.

CHÆREPHON.

A Kingfisher do you call it? This is the first time I have chanced to hear its note. And to be sure it does sing in a most melancholy strain. How large a bird is it, Socrates?

---

in his voyage. His dead body being carried back to his wife, she leaped into the sea out of sympathy. They were afterwards both changed into birds, which the Greeks call Ἀλκυ-ονις, Kingfishers. Ovid. Met. XI. These birds, according to Pliny, make their nests in the middle of the sea, and breed in the winter, during which the weather is always calm. Hence the expression Halcyon days.

[a] Matre pulchra filia pulchrior. Hor.

SOCRATES.

The bird is not large, but large is the reward with which the Gods have honoured its conjugal fidelity. At the time of making its nest and hatching its young, the world enjoys Halcyon days, as the saying is. Though in the depth of winter, the weather is perfectly clear and serene; of which this day is a fair example. Do not you observe how very bright it is over head, and that the sea is unruffled with a single wave, its surface being every where as smooth as a looking-glass?

CHÆREPHON.

Right. This seems to be a Halcyon day; and so, I believe, yesterday was. But I must beg of you, Socrates, in the name of all the Gods, that you will be so good as to explain what you have been saying. How is it possible that women can be made of birds, or birds of women? Nothing, I think, can be much more incredible.

SOCRATES.

My dear Sir, you and I are very incompetent judges of what is possible and impossible. We trust to our own faculties to determine what is out of the reach of our ignorance, and blindly disbelieve because we cannot see. No wonder, therefore, that what is in reality easy enough, should often appear difficult; as that, to which we may very well attain, seems altogether inaccessible. Our inexperience, like our infancy, is thus frequently imposed on. For every man, even the very oldest, may be considered as a babe; since his age is as nothing compared to eternity. How then, Chærephon, can any person thus totally unacquainted with the extent of the divine power, take upon him to prescribe limits to it, and tell us what is possible and what impossible? You saw what a storm there was the day before yesterday. Any body only considering the dreadful thunder and lightning, and the prodigious violence of the wind, might very well have been afraid, that the whole frame of nature was ready to fall in pieces. Yet a little while after, how wonderfully

fully still and serene was the face of the sky, as it still continues! And can you suppose it a work more arduous and difficult to produce serenity from turbulence, and make order out of disorder, than to change the form of a woman into that of a bird? Our little children, you know, who understand how to model clay or wax, can make at pleasure a great variety of figures from the same materials. And why should there be any difficulty in believing, that the Divine Power, which is so infinitely superior to all comparison with ours, can at any time effect such changes with all imaginable ease? How much, do you think, the whole atmosphere may exceed the extent of your body?

CHÆREPHON.

How should any man, Socrates, be able to express in words what he cannot conceive in idea?

SOCRATES.

We cannot any of us avoid observing the different degrees of strength and weakness, which are found in different men. The state of manhood, compared to an infant of a week old,

old, exhibits an amazing inequality in respect of abilities in almost every thing relating to human life, in whatever belongs to arts and manufactures, in every work of the hands, and contrivance of the head; nothing of all which can so much as enter into the imagination of an infant. The strength of a full-grown man is so far out of all proportion to that of new-born babes, that he would be able with all the ease in the world to master some thousands of them. Such is the law of our nature, that we are in our infancy destitute of every thing, and altogether insufficient for our own support. But, if one human being be so different from another, how may we imagine the universe to appear in comparison with our slender power, when that comparison is made by a mind adequate to it? I suppose most persons will be willing to allow, that, as much as the extent of the world exceeds the size of Socrates or Chærephon, so much its [a] power, wisdom, and understanding, may be fairly concluded to excel those faculties in us. To such persons as you and me many things are impossible, which

[a] Alluding to Plato's notion of the Anima Mundi.

to others are easy enough. To play on the
flute to such as are unskilled in musick, to read
and write to those who do not so much as
know a letter, would be a task not less difficult
than making women of birds, or birds of women. Nature lodges a little helpless animal in
a commodious cell, furnishes him with feet
and wings, dresses and adorns him with a variety of beautiful colours, and thus constitutes
the bee, the wise artificer of [*b*] heavenly honey. From eggs destitute of life and speech,
how many inhabitants of air, of land, of water,
does this same nature form, practising, as they
say, the documents of art divine! The power
of the immortal Gods being so great, and we
puny mortals so very blind as not to perceive
things great or little, ignorant even of what
daily happens before our own eyes, how can
we pretend to speak with confidence of any
thing? The Kingfisher and the Nightingale are
to us equally enigmatical. But the tradition
which I have received from my parents con-

[*b*] Protinus aerii mellis cælestia dona. Virg. Georg. 4.
Denique ex hoc (bove) putrefacto nasci dulcissimas apes
mellis matres, Varro de re rustica.

cerning thy songs, [*c*] O bird melodious melancholy, I will deliver down entire to my children. I will not fail to celebrate thy pious affection for thy husband, making my wives [*d*] Xantippe and Myrto well acquainted with it, and mentioning, amongst other particulars, the honour done thee by the Gods! You, I hope, Chærephon, will act in the same manner.

CHÆREPHON.

So it becomes me, Socrates. Your words carry a double force, which tend to establish the mutual regard of man and wife.

SOCRATES.

Well, let us take our leave of the Kingfisher. It is time to quit the [*e*] Phalerick meadow, and return to the city.

CHÆREPHON.

Very well, let us be gone.

[*c*] Sweet bird, that shun'st the noise of folly,
    Most musical, most melancholy.
                  Milton, speaking of the nightingale.
[*d*] Of these two wives of Socrates, Myrto is hardly known, not having made so much noise in the world as Xantippe.

[*e*] Phaleros, a fine meadow near Athens.

[*f*] Of the manner in which HISTORY
ought to be written.

I Have been told, my dear Philo, that, in
the reign of [*g*] Lyfimachus, the good
people of Abdera were afflicted with a
fingular kind of difeafe. All in general were
feized with a violent fever, which continued
without intermiffion till about the feventh day;
when fome of them were relieved by a copious
difcharge of blood from the noftrils, and others
by as plentiful a flow of fweat. However,
though the fever thus left them, fome effects
were produced by it extraordinary and whim-
fical enough. Their minds on a fudden became

[*f*] Lucian is generally inclined to fquander the parts of
fpeech; but he nowhere fcatters them about him with greater
profufion than in this piece, where the fenfe is wiredrawn to
the laft degree.

[*g*] After the death of Alexander, his dominions being divided, Lyfimachus, one of his captains, became king of
Thrace, in which was the city Abdera.

so enchanted with tragedy, that they roared out Iambicks, and utter'd all in recitative. The Andromeda of Euripides became a favourite monody, and the speech of Perseus was chanted out most melodiously. Then was the city replete with tragedians pale and lean, all made fit for their parts by the seven days sickness.

[*b*] Love, cruel king of God and men, was one of the fine flourishes which those heroes sounded forth without ceasing. Till, at the last, a severe winter coming on, deprived them of their poetry, and restored them to their senses. The cause of all this, in my opinion, was no other than Archelaus. Archelaus was a favourite player, who had exhibited the story of Andromeda in the middle of a very hot summer; so hot, that many persons, before they were well out of the theatre, were directly taken ill with a fever; while the fancied forms of Andromeda, Perseus, and Medusa, fluttered before their senses, and recalled their delighted

---

[*b*] See a fragment of the Andromeda of Euripides, of which this line makes a part, in Barnes's edition of that author.

attention to the strains of tragedy. If I may
be allowed to make a comparison; I think,
that a great part of our men of learning do
at present labour under a disorder not much
unlike that of Abdera. Not that they act
tragedies: they are too far gone to be contented with the decent [*i*] Iambicks composed
by others. Ever since the beginning of the
present commotions, the war [*k*] with the barbarians, and the loss sustained in Armenia, which
was followed by so many victories; ever since
those events took place, all mankind seems to
be employed in writing the history of them.
At every step you take there starts up a Thucydides, an Herodotus, or a Xenophon. And
if so many historians arise after an onset, what
doubt can any longer remain, that [*l*] war is
the universal parent? The hearing and seeing
of all this put me in mind of the [*m*] philosopher of Sinope. On the report of Philip's

[*i*] Iambick is the measure of the Greek Tragedies.
[*k*] This war is said to have commenced in the year of
Christ 161, and to have ended in 164.
[*l*] See Diogenes Laertius IX, 7.
  Discors concordia fœtibus apta est. Ovid.
[*m*] Diogenes.

advancing,

advancing, the people of Corinth were all alarmed, and every body was in motion. One did one thing, and another another, with all his might and main. One provided arms, another carried stones. One secured the foundations of the walls, another the battlements. And every body was very busy in something or other, very useful no doubt, and very necessary. Diogenes, being a spectator of all this bustle, and having nothing in all the world to do, as nobody thought of employing him, tucked up his remains of an old cloak, and, with great earnestness and application, rolled up and down the tub in which he dwelt backwards and forwards all over [n] Craneium. One of his friends enquiring into the occasion; "I roll my tub, replied Diogenes, that I may not be thought the only idle man in a place where such multitudes are so busily employed." In like manner, my dear friend, Philo, that I may not be the only silent man when every body else is so very free of his tongue, nor open my mouth without speaking, like a mute in a play, I have been thinking, that I too may

[n] A place near Corinth, where Diogenes taught his disciples.

as well roll my tub in the beft manner I am
able. Do not you be afraid of my undertaking
a hiftory; I have not fo much affurance as to
venture on a recital of facts. I know very well,
that my little tub is in too crazy a condition to
be rolled over the hard ftones, unlefs I had a
mind to gather it up in [*p*] fcraps, or fee a
piece knocked out of it by every pebble. I will
tell you then what I have refolved on, and how
far I intend to engage in the conteft, without
laying claim to any fhare of the danger. I find
myfelf juft wife enough to keep out of the
way of the [*q*] fmoke, and the waves [*q*], and
the cares [*q*], which befet a profeffed author.
I fhall juft offer a little advice, and fubmit to
the opinion of others a few fuggeftions hardly
more fufficient to entitle me to be named on
the occafion, than if I fhould expect to be
talked of as an architect merely from having
foiled my finger with mortar. Moft people
feem to think, that no rules whatever can be
neceffary for fuch an undertaking; but that,
if a man can only make known his own mind,

[*p*] ὄστρακα. The cafks of the ancients were ufually made
of clay.

[*q*] Hom. Od. M. 219.

he has no more need of directions for compofing a hiftory, than he has of being taught the [r] art of putting one leg before the other, of walking, or looking, or eating. 'You, however, know very well, that hiftory is not fo extremely eafy; but that it is, at leaft as much as any other, one of thofe literary purfuits, which requires the utmoft care and attention; efpecially if, as Thucydides fays, the author aims at immortality. At the fame time I am well convinced, that any advice of mine can be expected to influence only a very few. Thofe, who have already finifhed their work, and given it to the publick, are likely to confider me in a very odious light. After being fo much praifed, it would be mere madnefs to expect them to be induced by any arguments of mine to blot out or correct what has been ratified by learned approbation, and even depofited in the courts of princes. And yet I cannot think there can be any great harm in offering a few remarks, which, if they fhould meet with forgivenefs, may ferve our hiftorians, in cafe of another war, as a canon of criticifm on their

[r] A walking-mafter appears to have been a profeffion unknown in the time of Lucian.

own

own works. Not that there is any danger of
our being attacked after thus beating our enemies all round us. But other nations may not
be so secure. The Celtæ, for instance, may
fall upon the Getæ; or the Indians may chance
to attack the Bactrians. And if, after all, my
rules and opinions be not assented to, writers
can but continue to follow their own. And
why should that give me any more pain than it
would, to an industrious physician to see the
honest people of Abdera all out of their
senses again? As my intention is not only to
point out what should be carefully selected
for use, but also what is to be as faithfully
avoided, I shall first caution the writer of history how to keep clear of the latter. I shall
direct him in what manner to proceed straight
forward without interruption, how he is to set
out, and what order he is to observe in his
progress, how he is to moderate his conduct,
what he may pass over in silence, where he is
to be very particular and circumstantial, what
he may skim slightly over, and how the whole
is to be connected, and expressed in language
the most plain and perspicuous. In this manner

nor my purpose is to conduct him to the end
of his work. Let us now touch on the most
usual blemishes of inferior authors. It would
be tedious, as well as foreign to my design,
minutely to examine the faults common to
every species of composition, with regard to
the language, the congruity, the sentiment, and
whatever else may be the result of ignorance
and unskilfulness in the art. These common
faults, as has been observed, consist in the un-
aptness and incongruity of expression. I have
had many opportunities of knowing; and, if
you will bestow any considerable degree of
your attention, I believe, you will readily agree
with me concerning the several particulars in
which historians most frequently fail. By way
of specimen, it may not be unseasonable to
produce a few known examples, the better to
illustrate my meaning. First of all, let us take
notice of the error so unpardonable, and yet
at the same time so prevailing, when the writer,
neglecting to give an exact narrative of facts,
bestows his whole time and pains in exalting
at any rate the characters of his princes and generals; extolling the actions of his own countrymen as much above the truth, as he under-
values

values and degrades thofe of the enemy. As
if Hiftory were not a province very feparate
and diftinct from panegyrick! between which
a vaft boundary is placed, filling up, as a
mufician might fay, all the interval of a double
diapafon! The panegyrift has no other care,
than by a profufe heap of indifcriminate praife
to gratify the vanity of his hero; regardlefs
how many lies he may find it neceffary to tell,
in order to attain his end. While Hiftory allows not the flighteft deviation from truth
in the fmalleft circumftance: juft as the wind-
pipe (fo any fmatterer in phyfick will inform
you) cannot fafely admit the leaft particle of
what we eat or drink. Such writers as we
are fpeaking of feem not to confider, that the
rules and ends of hiftory are very different
from thofe of Poetry. In Poetry we are made
to expect the moft unbounded licence, unre-
ftrained by any one law befides the good-will
and pleafure of the poet; who, when filled
with the divine afflatus, and having all the
mufes at his elbow, may befpeak a fet of
winged horfes, for his chariot, which he may
order to prance upon the furface of the water,

or

or trip on the [*] ears of the standing corn. All this the poet may do without danger of censure. More than this, he may make a shew of the great and mighty Jove hoisting up earth and sea fastened together by a chain, which the amazed spectators are horribly afraid will break, and let all tumble down and be dashed to pieces together. This he may do, if he pleases; nobody will say a word against it. He is at liberty to bestow on his favourite [†] Agamemnon a head and eyes like Jupiter's, a breast like brother Neptune's, a belt like that of Mars; in short he may lay all the Cœlestials under

---

[*] Hom. Il. XX. 227.
These lightly skimming, when they swept the plain,
Nor ply'd the grass, nor bent the tender grain;
And when along the level seas they flew,
Scarce on the surface curl'd the briny dew.
         Pope's Translation.
Imitated by Virgil. Æn. VII. 805.
    Camilla
Outstript the wind in speed upon the plain,
Flew o'er the fields, nor hurt the bearded grain:
She swept the seas; and, as she skimm'd along,
Her flying feet unbath'd in billows hung.
         Dryden's Translation.
[†] Hom. Il. B. 478.

[*u*] contribution, for the purpose of equipping the son of Atreus and Aerope; especially as no one individual of them all, neither Jupiter, nor Neptune, nor Mars, nor any body, can of himself equal in all respects the accomplished Agamemnon. History, when it aspires to flattery of this kind, becomes a kind of poetical prose at best, silent the muses' tongue sublime, yet participating of the marvellous, though without the enchanting numbers; for which very reason the prodigious becomes the more strongly marked. How very capital a defect is it then to be incapable of separating the provinces of prose and verse, arraying history in the meretricious attire of poesy, and daubing it with every extravagance of fable and flattery! Just as if you were to take a sturdy wrestler, stout as an oak, dress him in purple, rub his face with rouge and white lead, and bestow on him other ornaments equally in character; what a ridiculous figure, O Hercules, would you make of him! However, I do not pretend

---

[*u*] To paint his Venus, auld Appelles
Wal'd a' the bonny maids of Greece.

Allan Ramsay.

to say, that no kind of praise is ever to be endured in history. I only say, that it must be seasonably introduced, and used with moderation. It is never to be such as may prove irksome to the reader, never dissonant from those rules of practice, which I proceed to give. Those who, taking it into their heads to divide history into two parts, the useful and delectable, do therefore introduce panegyrick as a recreation for the reader, which belongs to their second division, you will allow to be very egregiously mistaken in forming such an unwarrantable distinction; the sole business and end of History being utility, arising from truth alone. If indeed it should prove attended with delight, as a champion may chance to have beauty, it is so much the better. But if not, there is no lawful impediment to prevent the generous Nicostratus [y], son of Isidotus, descended from Hercules, from being superior to both his competitors; although not the handsomest man in the world. Nor is there any reason why Alcæus, the beautiful Milesian, should not

[y] Commentators differ concerning the pedigree of Nicostratus. To their learned enquiries nothing can here be added. *Non nostrum est tantas componere lites.*

contend

contend with him, who was, as it is said, a favourite of his. History, chancing to pick up pleasure by the way, must doubtless have many lovers; but, while solely intent on its one great end, the publishing of truth, will have little leisure to attend to ornament. Besides, it may be added, that nothing in History can afford much pleasure, which carries with it the appearance of fable, and which will go very ill down, unless you should regard as your judges the very dregs of the people. The minutest impropriety will not escape the discerning and rigid critick, than whom Argus himself, though eyes all over, was not more sharp-sighted, nor curious and inquisitive. Such readers examine every word by weight and measure, rejecting without mercy whatever is found adulterate; and not less careful to retain whatever is approved, legitimate, accurate, and exact. Such are the readers a writer should constantly have in his eye, to their judgment he is to appeal, without coveting the extravagant applauses, which criticks of a different cast may be induced to bestow. But if, indifferent to the opinions of the judicious, you should at all events resolve on exhibiting

a history

a history highly seasoned with panegyrick, fable, and other false ornaments, your work must make just such a becoming figure as Hercules exhibited in Lydia; where, you know, he was the most humble servant of his mistress Omphale. Doubtless you have seen the formidable hero depicted in a dress not altogether Herculean. Omphale has flung the lion's skin over her delicate shoulder, while her lily hand grasps the club. Hercules, who is very busy at his spinning, is attired in purple and saffron, and chastised, as he richly deserves, with a blow of Omphale's slipper. How ridiculous is the idea excited by such a picture, where the dress so badly fits and so ill adorns the wearer! The man divine is sunk into something less than woman! And yet, it is possible, such a taste may prevail. But the judicious few, whom you consider as nobody, cannot but laugh at so incongruous, so unapt, so discordant a composition. There resides in each particular object its own peculiar grace; which being removed from its proper situation, use and beauty perish. Praise, indeed, may be very agreeable to the man on whom it is bestowed, though to all others nauseous enough; especially when it is given to that monstrous excess in use with the mob of authors, who observe so little moderation in their manner of soliciting the good will of their patrons, that flattery, so very bare-faced, is conspicuous to every eye. Without method or sense to conceal their adulation, having once set out, they rush on through every thing in their way, heedless of the reader, who is thus bemired in all the depth of absurd and palpable lies. By these means, who can wonder if they fail to attain what they so eagerly pursue? For what man of sound sense does not hate and abhor such wretched sycophants? Aristobulus had undertaken an account of the single combat between Alexander and Porus, which part of his book he particularly chose to read to the conqueror, as they sailed together on the river Hydaspes, not without much expectation of favour for the many valiant acts, which he had falsly attributed to the hero. But Alexander greatly disappointed his lying panegyrist, by suddenly snatching the book from his hand, and flinging it at the author's head. As it fell into the river, the king observed, that the historian was highly worthy of accompanying his work, for having fought so stout a battle a battle for him, and made him throw his dart through so many elephants. Alexander was equally right in not enduring with any temper the assuming [z] Architect, who proposed to make a statue of him out of Mount Athos. Being offended with such gross adulation, he no longer encouraged him as an artist. And what man can take delight in such praises, unless he be so thoroughly stupid as not to perceive what nobody else can avoid seeing immediately? Silly women and ugly beaux may insist on being drawn as finished pieces, from a persuasion, that their looks will be im-

[a] The name of that bold designer was Dinocrates. He was extremely desirous of being known to Alexander, which he could not find any way of bringing about, till he hit upon the following expedient. Having besmeared himself with oil, with a crown of poplar on his head, and a lion's skin on his shoulders, without other dress, he contrived to throw himself in the monarch's way. His majesty, tickled with the novelty of the appearance, was graciously pleased to laugh, and his retinue followed the royal example. Some accounts say the courtiers laughed first; but that is not probable. However, the man's expectations were answered, and by proper degrees Dinocrates was received into favour. But, behold! in process of time, he fell a sacrifice to the excess of those thriving arts, by which he had been exalted. Hear this, ye hangers-on, and fawn with moderation!

Z 2 proved

proved in proportion as the painter lays on his colours. Thus the common herd of authors, having in view only the time prefent, think of nothing befides what they conceive to be their own immediate intereft; for which they deferve to be heartily defpifed, as their coarfe and aukward flattery is now apparent to every body, and cannot fail at any time of rendering all they fay fufpected. But if the writer is firmly perfuaded, that there ought at any rate to be in hiftory a mixture of the pleafant, let him fpread over his work thofe ornaments only which are ftrictly confiftent with an adherence to truth: from the neglect of which it happens, that fo very many are induced to fay fo very much nothing at all to the pnrpofe. I will now proceed to give an account, as well as I can remember, of what I have [a] lately heard from the hiftorians in Ionia; and not in Ionia only, but alfo in Achaia, relating the fe-

[a] M. de Soul is almoft in raptures with this "*lately*," from which he difcovers the exact time of Lucian's returning home from his travels into Italy and Gaul. It appears, he fays, very plainly, that he muft have been in Ionia about the year of Chrift 163, after an abfence from his native country of twelve years at leaft.

veral

veral incidents of this same war. By all the
Graces, I beseech you not to refuse your assent
to what I am going to say, to the truth of
which I could swear with great safety, were it
decent to swear upon paper. One of my authors begins with addressing himself to the
Muses, earnestly intreating the Goddesses to be
propitious, and lend him a hand. A most
hopeful beginning of his history! Presently
my gentleman compares his hero to Achilles,
and the king of the Persians to Thersites;
without once reflecting, that our prince would
have got more credit by killing Hector than
Thersites [b]. To put the warrior to flight,
who had before driven so many brave men
before him, would have been something more
worthy of recording. The historian then drops
a hint concerning his own [c] merit; and what
a fortunate circumstance it was for such illustrious actions to be immortalized by so great a
genius! In the progress of his work he takes
occasion to say something in favour of his native country Miletus, not forgetting to repre-

[b] Hom. Il. xxii, 158.
[c] Arrian introduces his history of the great actions of
Alexander, with a panegyrick upon himself.

hend

hend the negligence of Homer in that particular, who has nowhere thought good to inform us where he was born. Towards the end of his poem he promises in so many plain words, that he will make the most of our exploits, and at the same time depress the Barbarians as much as lies in his power. Beginning his history, he thus recounts the causes of the war: "That villain Vologesus," says he, "that rascal—plague take him! began the war for no better reason than this." And in no better a manner than this our author proceeds. Another, a zealous disciple of Thucydides, and most devoutly wishing to imitate his great original, that he may exhale the sweet odour of Attica, and set out in the best manner imaginable, begins with the venerable mention of his own dear name. Thus he [d]: Creperius Calpurnianus, the Pompeiopolitanian, composed the history of the war between the Parthians and Romans, shewing how they fought, and beginning as they began."—After this I need not tell you how he goes on; the harangues he makes in Armenia, by the aid

[a] Thucydides begins his history in this manner.

of the [*e*] Corcyræan orator; how he sends a pestilence amongst the people of [*f*] Nisibis, for not siding with the Romans;—in short how the man takes every thing from Thucydides, excepting only his [*g*] *Pelasgick* and his [*b*] *long walls*, which were, it seems, the residence of those afflicted with the pestilence. Advancing from [*i*] Æthiopia, he makes a descent into Ægypt, and visits the extensive territories of the king, where he does mighty well to stop. For my part, I took my leave of him, while he was burying the poor [*k*] Athenians at Nisibis, knowing very well what he would say after I left him. You must understand it is

[*e*] See Thucydides.
[*f*] A city of Mesopotamia.
[*g*] A place in which the Athenians deemed it infamous to live; which scruple was however overcome by the necessities of a siege. See Thucydides.
[*h*] See Thucydides.
[*i*] It is in this manner Thucydides traces out the progress of the plague of Athens, thus copied by the plague of History. Dr. Mead was induced to believe, that the plague is constantly of African original, and is spread only by contagion to other parts of the world. See Mead's works, Quarto edition, p. 246.
[*k*] Meaning Romans, who are here called Athenians by courtesy of history.

commonly thought a very meritorious copying of Thucydides to turn his littlenesses to your own purpose; as for instance, in such phrases as these: *as a body may say; not for the same reason, believe me—I had almost forgot to mention*, &c. &c. This writer has given us several Roman names of arms and machines made use of in war, and talks of such things as ditches and bridges in the same terms they do. Think with yourself how very like he is to Thucydides, and what a dignity it gives to Grecian history to interlard it with Latin names, patching on here and there a bit of purple, the better to preserve grace and uniformity! Another creeps on in a low commentary, hardly superior to what might be supposed to be the work of a common carpenter, or foot-soldier, or sutler that follows the camp. This man truly may be very well endured, as he at once appears to be what he really is. And at any rate he has laid in a stock of materials, which may afford good employment to some future writer of sufficient capacity for such an undertaking. What I blamed him for was, that his title was so very pompous in comparison of his work: " The

Parthian

Parthian History, composed by Callimorphus, the physician to the sixth regiment of pikemen." Answerable to this the number of each book was orderly marked at the end. And he concludes his introduction, which is more than commonly frigid, with informing us, that it is quite familiar to a physician to compose a history; inasmuch as Æsculapius is the son of Apollo, and Apollo is the commanding officer of the muses, and prince of all instruction. He begins in the Ionick dialect, but all at once, I know not why, changes it for that which is in common use. [*l*] After οἱρεσιν and [*l*] πειρην and [*l*] οκοσα and [*l*] νωσοι, he gives as such expressions as are in every body's mouth, and may be heard in every street. If I am to take notice of a learned work lately published at Corinth, far exceeding all expectation, I shall only touch on the author's design, without mentioning his name. In his beginning, in the very first sentence of his preface, he attacks the reader with [*m*] interrogations, having all the desire

in

[*l*] Words in the Ionick dialect.

[*m*] One method of arguing a matter, as practised by the ancient logicians, was by asking questions, pressing your antagonist

in the world to shew the wisdom of his method, and to prove that none other than a wise man ought to undertake the writing of history. Then after a while comes syllogism upon syllogism. In short, his proem is nothing else but a bundle of questions in every species of argumentation. There is a surfeit of flattery, an importunity of praise, all the ensnaring art of the sycophant, wrapped up in syllogism and interrogatory. What vexed me was, to hear a philosopher with a long grey beard set out with remarking what a happy circumstance it was for our prince to have philosophers deign to record his greatness. If it be really so, thought I, the philosopher might leave his readers to find it out, without telling us so himself. I must not forget the exordium of him who says, "I am going to [n] speak of the Romans and Parthians;" and lower down, "But it was fit that the Persians should have the worst of it;" and again, "This was Osroes, whom the Greeks

---

tagonist with one after another, till you drive him up into a corner, where he is obliged to surrender at discretion. Socrates was the first who thus catechised his disciples. See Spectator, N°. 239.

[n] See Herodotus.

call

call Oxyrhoes;" with a great deal more of the
same kind. You see there is a resemblance between the two; only this man copies Herodotus, as the other did Thucydides. Another
scholar of Thucydides even outdoes his master,
describing, as he thinks, with all the perspicuity and elegance and strength of language,
every city, every mountain, every field, and
every river, that comes in his way. " May
the averter of evils turn all this on the heads
of our enemies!" Far less cold are the Caf-
pian snows and the Gallick ice, than the conceits of such a head! A whole book scarcely
suffices for a description of the general's shield;
" the [o] Gorgon on the boss, azure eyes,
white and black, a girdle like the rainbow,
the snakes twisted and curled!" The breeches
of Vologesus, the bridle of his horse, how
many thousand heroick words do they employ!
Such were the [p] locks of Osroes swimming
across the Tibris! Into a cave he escaped,
where ivy and myrtle and laurel laid their heads
so lovingly together, as to compose an exact
an exquisite shade! without such necessary helps

[o] Hom. Il. Δ. 36. and E. 741.
[p] See Spanhemius, 450.

as thefe, you fee, it would be impoffible to comprehend any thing recorded in hiftory! From an ignorance of the fubject, and an inability to do juftice to it, they turn afide to caves and regions untrodden, where they may indulge their talents for [q] idle defcription. Great events crowd the way; but fuch hiftorians are like the rich man, who was the other day a fervant. He has juft fucceeded to his mafter's eftate, and finds his riches fo ftrange and uncouth, that he neither knows what victuals to eat, or what clothes to wear. Though birds and hares and boars are all before him, he fingles out pulfe and faltfifh; with which, being his old acquaintance, he ftuffs himfelf till he is ready to fplit. Nothing is too improbable, nothing too [r] abfurd for our hifto-

---

[q] Where pure defcription held the place of fenfe.

Pope.

[r] The poet Lucan furnifhes many laughable inftances of what is here expofed. In the fea-fight of Marfeilles, the firft man that is killed is pierced at the fame inftant by two fpears; one in his back, and the other in his breaft, the two points meeting exactly in the middle. The foul drives out each of the fpears, and flies out of his body, half at one wound, and half at the other. See Lucan's Pharfalia, and Spence's Polymetis, p. 30.

rian.

rian. He makes a man inſtantly expire by a wound in his great toe. Nay, the general Priſcus did but call out luſtily, and ſtraightway there fell down dead full ſeven and twenty of the enemy. In recounting the numbers of the ſlain, the letters of the [1] commanders to their maſter do not match him for lying. There fell of the enemy, ſays he, at the city [*] Europus, three hundred and ſeventy thouſand two hundred and ſix; of the Romans only two were killed, and nine wounded. This, I fancy, is rather too much for a ſober man to ſwallow. I have another obſervation to make worthy of ſome attention. From an extravagant paſſion for Attick purity he has thought fit to turn the Latin names into Greek. He very gravely calls Saturninus Κρονιος; Fronto, Φροντις; Titian, Τιτανιος, &c. &c. Speaking of Severianus, he tells us, thoſe perſons are greatly miſtaken, who attribute his death to the ſword; for he died of hunger. He choſe

---

[1] Meaning, perhaps, the letters of Priſcus and Caſſius to the Emperor Verus, in whoſe reign the empire was attacked on almoſt every ſide. Verus himſelf went in perſon againſt Vologeſus, king of the Parthians.

[*] In Media.

this for him, it seems, as the easiest death; not considering at the same time, that it was all over with him in three days; whereas there are few perhaps who could not have lived without food for a whole week. Unless it should be supposed, that Osroes was to stand by in waiting till Severianus expired, who for that reason was too complaisant to hold out any longer. I know not what to make, my friend Philo, of those historians who adopt the language of poetry. [*u*] "Mighty was the crash of the murmuring machine." "Down thundered the tumbling wall." Again, in another part of the celebrated work: "Edessa rattling around with clanging arms, all was tumult, noise, and dreadful din." "The general was divided in his aim, nor knew how best to storm the fated wall." Meanwhile in the very mid-

---

[*u*] Hom. II. A. 530. B. 3. 210. A. 504.

Αυτοῖς δ᾽ εἴσω, ἀραβησε δε τευχε᾽ επ᾽ αυτω.

Ponderous he falls; his clanging arms resound;
And his broad buckler rings against the ground.
        Pope's Translation.

He was a swinging fat fellow, and fell with almost as much noise as a house. His tobacco-box dropt at the same time from his pocket.
        Tom Jones, B. IV. c. 8.

dle of all this grandeur, up pops the vileſt word imaginable. Language fit for the uſe of the loweſt beggar, and only to be expected from the meaneſt man alive, creeps into a niche of the ſublime. " The corporal wrote a letter to his officer." " The ſoldiers bought belly-timber." " They waſhed, and were there in a crack." &c. &c. This motley ſtyle reminds us of the player, one of whoſe feet ſtruts in a moſt ſtately buſkin, while the other is moſt humbly tied in a ſandal. Some there are who preſent us with ſo very pompous and heroical a preface, extended to ſo immoderate a length, that you cannot have the leaſt doubt of finding every circumſtance recorded with the greateſt exactneſs in the body of the work; which, notwithſtanding, turns out to be an inſignificant pitiful production, a child peeping through the maſk of a giant. On ſuch an occaſion who can forbear applying the old Adage? [x] The mountains were in labour, and have brought forth a mouſe. In hiſtory every thing

[x] The mountain in labour is now no more to be found in the fables of Æſop. Moſes du Soul,

ſhould

should have the same complexion; all should be of a piece. The head must answer to the body, as the body to the head. After a golden helmet, who would not laugh to see a breastplate composed of rags and patches of rotten leather? Can our hero be well shielded with twigs of willow, or well booted with hog-skin? And yet, nothing is more common than to give to a dwarf the head of the [y] Rhodian Colossus. While on the contrary, you sometimes meet with a history all body and no head, no preface, nothing to prepare you for the narration. Such authors have Xenophon and others of the ancients in their eye, whose manner they imitate, as they think. Xe-

[v] Every child can tell the story of the Colossus of Rhodes, which he has seen in a picture-stall striding over the mainmast of a ship. It was in height 105 feet. Chares Lyndius, a scholar (an apprentice, I suppose) of Lysippur, was the maker, who, after working a dozen years upon it, finished it in the year before Christ 278. After standing 56 years it was thrown down by an earthquake, and lay prostrate till the year of Christ 672, when Rhodes being taken by the Saracens, it was sold. Though no doubt it must have suffered very considerable motilations, there was then brass enough of it left to load 900 camels, allowing to each camel 900 pounds weight.

nophon,

nophon, you know, lets us into this secret in
his very first line, that Darius and his wife Pa-
ryfatis had two sons. But Xenophon knew very
well, though our authors do not, that there
are certain circumstances, in the mention of
which is included all that is essential to a preface, without making that appearance in the
eyes of the undiscerning, as we shall shew presently. But to tell such enormous untruths
concerning the distance and situation of places,
to make mistakes of whole parasangs and days
journeys, what excuse can be alledged for this?
One gentleman has conducted his story in so
slovenly a manner, that he seems never to have
had the advantage of conferring with [z] Syrus,
nor to have been a member of the privy council held in a [a] barber's shop. Speaking of
the city Europus, he thus expresses himself:
" Europus founded by the people of Edessa,
is situated in Mesopotamia, at the distance of
two stages from the Euphrates." Not con-

[z] Xenephon's Expedition of Cyrus.
[a] Syrus, I suppose, was a great man's butler. Nobody
wants to be told what a world of information may be obtained
from a great man's butler in a barber's shop.

tented with this, the obliging man hoists up my native Samosata, citadel, walls and all, and carries it over to [*b*] Mesopotamia, where he sets it down between two rivers, which he makes to flow by on each side as near as may be without washing the walls of the city. How idle therefore, my friend Philo, would it be for me any longer to dispute my being a Parthian, or to deny my being a Mesopotamian, after this author has laid violent hands upon me, dragged me from my home, and enrolled my name in the city in which he liked best to have me born! What he says and swears of Severianus is most highly probable; which he declares he had from one of those who escaped from the battle. It was his determined resolution, he assures us, not to die by sword, or poison, or halter; but to invent some death tragical and new. As it happened, he had cups of very fine glass, and of a very uncommon size; and, death being finally resolved on, he broke the largest of them, and cut his throat with one of the fragments. Such

[*b*] A country in the middle of Asia between two rivers (as the name denotes), Tigris on the east, and Euphrates on the west.

was the hero's heroical end, effected without poniard or spear! Then, since [c] Thucydides pronounced a funeral oration on those that were first slain in the war, our ingenious author concludes, that he must needs say something of the same kind concerning Severianus. Though poor Thucydides is as innocent as a lamb of what passed in Armenia, yet they all set their faces against Thucydides! Accordingly, after treating Severianus with a most magnificent funeral, he mounts me up upon his grave one Afranius Silo, a centurion, and rival of Pericles, who makes so pompous a speech, and says of him so many fine things, that (forgive me, ye Graces! ye Graces, forgive me!) I laughed till the tears came. What mortal could stand by unmoved, when the eloquent Afranius, plenteously weeping as he wound up the bottom of his oration, and setting up a most heart-piercing howl, so feelingly lamented the sumptuousness of his suppers, not forgetting the many healths so jovial a fellow had formerly put about? The second Ajax then gives the finishing stroke. Standing by the grave, in Afranius's best manner, and most

[c] Thucydides, B. II.

nobly

nobly drawing his fword, he flays himfelf in
the fight of them all; well deferving, O Mars,
long before to have perifhed, if ever before he
uttered fuch a fpeech! He adds, all that were
prefent at this fpectacle, admired and extolled
Afranius. For my part, although the orator
was fo well affected to foups and platters, and
though he had even wept at the bare mention of cheefecakes, I could not help condemn-
ing him in other refpects. Particularly I
blamed him for not having, before he died
himfelf, firft put to death the author of the
ftory. I could produce abundance of fuch examples. But, having mentioned thefe few,
I proceed to the other part of my defign;
which was, to confider by what means an author
might be enabled to write better. Authors
there are, who from ignorance, and want of
tafte, from neither knowing what to fay, nor
when to be filent, either wholly omit,
or flightly pafs over, in the utmoft hurry,
fuch great actions as fhould command their utmoft attention; meanwhile they moft copioufly
and carefully tire us with a minute detail of
the moft arrant trifles. Juft as if a man, unable

able to comprehend in his ideas the Olympian
Jove, and blind to the beauty and grandeur of
the whole, should never once think of either
praising or mentioning any more of it than
merely the fine [*d*] pedestal, with an exact
description of which he pesters all manner of
persons! I am acquainted with a writer of history, who scarcely condescended to bestow half
a dozen lines on the battle at [*e*] the Europus,
and yet thought nothing of wasting above
twenty measures of [*f*] water, before he was
pleased to relieve us from an impertinent story,
which no way in the world concerned us.
" There was a certain Moorish knight, Mau-

[*d*] Many persons here understand the word κρηπις to
mean slipper, an interpretation with which Gronovius is
greatly scandalized. He has seen Jupiter Olympius on an
old coin, without a rag to his back, bare-footed and bare-
legged, and cries out shame on all such as go about to insinuate, that Jupiter ever was master of any such thing as a
slipper!

[*e*] A river of Macedonia.

[*f*] Of old, Lawyers and others used to measure their
speeches by a kind of water-clock, answering the purpose of
an hour-glass, which last, about a century ago, was an appendix to an English pulpit, and enabled the congregation to take
measure of the sermon.

facas by name, who, wandering hungry and dry over the mountains, had the good fortune to light on some Syrian boors, who gave him a dinner. At first indeed they were somewhat afraid of him; but, when they found that he meant no harm, they considered him as a friend, and treated him accordingly. As good luck would have it, one of these Syrians had travelled in the land of the Moors, where a brother of his was a soldier." Then, after a deal of other tedious stuff, he tells us a long-winded story of " his hunting in Mauritania, that he saw great numbers of Elephants feeding peaceably together in a pasture, that he narrowly escaped being devoured by a monstrous lion, and what huge fishes they were which he purchased at Cæsaræa." Our admirable historian, not troubling himself about the great slaughter at the Europus, making no mention of the various attacks, the necessary truces, nor the advanced guards on each side, is detained till late in the evening, in taking a full view of Malchio, the Syrian, who is buying prodigious fine [g] chars at Cæsaræa al-

[g] Winander-Mere is by no means the only water in the world, in which the Char has been caught.

most

moſt for nothing. Night coming on, I ſuppoſe, prevented his ſtaying ſupper; for the fiſhes were dreſt and ready to come upon table. If all this had not been ſo carefully recorded, of what important matters muſt we have remained ignorant! It would have been a moſt grievous loſs to the Romans, and which they could but ill have borne, had Mauſacas, the thirſty Moor, found nothing to drink, and been obliged to return ſupperleſs to the camp! As I mean not to make you laugh, I ſay nothing of the female piper that came to them from the neighbouring village. I omit any mention of their mutual [b] preſents, how the Moor gave Malchio a lance, and how Malchio made Mauſacas a preſent of a button; with many other circumſtances of almoſt equal conſequence, which the battle at the Europus gave occaſion to. May it not be ſaid of ſuch authors, that they ſpy not the roſes, though they prick their fingers with the thorns? There is a man, my Philo, who has often made me laugh, nor ſhall I eaſily forget him; who, without ever having ſet a foot in Corinth, or having been

[b] Hom. Il. H. 299.

as far from home as Cenchræa, without having once seen Syria or Armenia, does notwithstanding thus begin: " The ear" (says my sententious gentleman) " the ear is less faithful than the eye. I trust not to hearsay, nor do I write save that which I have seen." With such great accuracy had he seen and examined every thing he writes of, that he tells us the Parthian dragons (which are no other than their standards borne in war, one of which always goes before a thousand men) " the Parthian dragons," says he, " are of an enormous size, bred in Persia, a little above Iberia. At first, he says, they are carried aloft in the air, fastened to long poles, striking terror at a distance, which increases as they advance. But, when the battle begins, and the soldiers come to action, then the dragons are all untied, and let go against the enemy. The sure consequence of which is, that great numbers of our people lose their lives by them. They fold themselves round a man's body, and belabour him, till they beat the breath out of him." Our author is enabled to be the more positive as to all this, because he had the precaution to get up upon a high tree, where he was perfectly

fectly safe, and saw all that passed. It was very happy for us, that he was stationed at so convenient a distance from such dangerous monsters; otherwise we might have had to lament the loss of our admirable historian, whose own personal prowess was nevertheless distinguished in the war by many illustrious actions. His farthest way about being his nearest way home, he underwent full many a peril, and was wounded near [*i*] Sura, on his march from [*k*] Cranium to [*l*] Lerna. This history was recited in the hearing of the Corinthians, a people all assured that their well-informed author had not so much as seen the war in a picture on a wall; who knew for certain, that he was totally unacquainted with arms, ignorant of every machine made use of in war, and a perfect stranger to all martial

[*i*] A town of Cælosyria, on the banks of the Euphrates.

[*k*] A grove of Peloponnesus, near Corinth, famous for being the residence of Diogenes and his tub.

[*l*] A lake near Argos, in Peloponnesus, where Hercules slew the Hydra. The reader will judge for himself, whether the nearest way from Cranium to Lerna is to go by Sura:

    Cranium.

Lerna.   Sura,

terms,

terms, as well as to the manner of difpofing an army. He knows not fo much as what is meant by [*m*] a phalanx broad in front and narrow in flank, or narrow in front and broad in flank; nor is he able to diftinguifh which is the van, and which is the wing. One good man has favoured us with a full account from beginning to end of all the tranfactions in Armenia, Syria, Mefopotamia, at the Tigris, and in Media. And, having done all this in lefs than the compafs of five hundred lines, he calls it writing a hiftory. His title is almoft as long as his book: " The hiftory of the feveral exploits lately performed by the Romans in Armenia, Mefopotamia, and Media; written by Antiochanus, who came off conqueror in the games facred to Apollo." I fuppofe he had been the winner in a race, when he was a boy, which might furnifh a pretence for this piece of vanity. I have met with another [*n*] author ftill more daring, who undertakes to record events before they come to pafs. Before any

[*m*] See the ηθιη ςα᾽αι ξ and πλαγια ϛαλαγξ in Potter's Antiquities, vol. II. p. 58.
[*n*] Suppofed to mean Jamblichus.

fuch

such thing has happened, he makes us acquainted with the captivity of [*o*] Vologesus, and the killing of [*o*] Osroes, who was exposed to a very fierce lion; and, above all, what a glorious triumph we enjoyed upon the occasion. Thus inspired with prophetick fury, and having every thing his own way, he hurries on to the end of his work. He has built a city in Mesopotamia, most great in greatness, most beautiful in beauty. Of this only he still doubts and deliberates, whether he shall call his city the city of Victory, the city of Concord, or the city of Peace. Till that is determined, this most beautiful city, so overflowing with all manner of nonsense, must continue without a name. He has not only undertaken to tell us beforehand whatever is to be done in India, but has taken under his protection the navigation of the more distant coast. This Indian adventure of his, which otherwise might seem premature, is actually begun. He has already transported over the river Indus, under the

[*o*] A Parthian king, contemporary with Nero. See Tacitus.

[*p*] General Osroes has been mentioned before.

command

command of Caffius, the third Legion, the
Celtæ, and a small body of the Mauri. What
they are to do there, and how they will sustain
the shock of the elephants, we shall know in a
little time, as soon as our admirable author
shall have time to send us a letter from
[q] Musuris or [q] Oxydracæ. In this pre‐
posterous manner do those persons continually
babble, who never saw themselves one single
incident worth remembering; and who, if they
had, were utterly incapable of describing it
to others. In reality they know nothing, but
are always ready to rack their brains, if they
had any brains to rack, in the production of
whatever impertinence may be supposed to
employ an idle tongue. Such authors take un‐
common pains to be orthodox in the [r] num‐
ber of their books, and are most classically nice
in their titles; which last are sometimes laugh‐
able enough. One gives us so many books of
the Parthian victories. Then, because forsooth
there is the [s] Atthis, we must have books

[q] In India, on this side the Ganges.
[r] A childishness from which even the author of Paradise
Lost was not exempt.
[s] Written by Philochorus.

the

the firſt and ſecond of the Parthis. However, I have read an author, who outdoes them all. What other title, though ever ſo fine, can compare with the Parthoniciks of Demetrius Sagalaſſenſis? Believe me, I mention not ſuch choice compoſitions merely for the ſake of raiſing a ſimile. I think them uſeful examples of what a writer ſhould take care to avoid; who, if he can keep clear of ſuch faults as I have pointed out to him, will be in the way of doing ſomething very conſiderable towards writing well. Indeed he may be ſaid to enjoy almoſt every advantage, if what the Dialecticks teach be true, that [1], of two things which have no medium, the removal of the one is the eſtabliſhment of the other. "Well now, you will ſay to me, you have cleared the ground, cut down the briars and thorns, carried off the rubbiſh, and made all ſmooth and level, let us ſee what kind of an edifice you yourſelf are able to raiſe. You have ſhewn

[1] Of things without a medium life and death are an example; of things with a medium white and black. Whatever is not mortal is immortal. But, becauſe an author's coat is not black, it does by no means follow, that therefore it muſt be white.

yourſelf

yourself a very brave fellow in demolishing the works of others, it very well becomes you to exhibit a specimen of your own, and you would act prudently in producing something so super-excellent, that even Momus himself may have nothing to object to it."—Then, Sir, I begin with observing, that whoever wishes to attain the dignity of a genuine historian, must not by any means whatever be unprovided with these two principal articles, political sagacity, and adequate powers of expressing himself. The former, being the gift of nature, cannot otherwise be obtained. But, by great labour and pains, and an unwearied assiduity in the study of the ancients, a great degree of eloquence may be acquired. It is obvious, that what is beyond the reach of art cannot be mended by any advice of mine. This little tract does not pretend to teach wisdom and discernment where nature has denied them. If indeed that could be done, no pains whatever should be spared to effect it. Who could grudge the expence of making gold out of lead, or silver out of tin? Which would not be a task more arduous and extraordinary than to make

make a [u] Titormus of a [x] Conon, or a [y] Milo of a [z] Leotrophides. Art and design cannot be supposed to create materials, but only to teach the proper use of them. Neither Iccus, nor Prodicus, nor Theon, nor any other learned professor of gymnasticks,

[u] Titormus, according to Ælian, was a sturdy cowherd, whom Milo, who was not a little vain of his own exploits, chanced to meet with, and challenged to make a trial of his strength. Titormus modestly observed, that his strength was very inconsiderable. However, to oblige Milo, he pulled off his coat, and taking a huge stone out of the river, played with it for some time on the ground, then raised it to his knee; afterwards to his shoulders, carried it on his back about twenty yards, and then tossed it away. Milo meanwhile could only stare, for he was scarcely able to move it. Titormus then laid hold of two very strong and fierce bulls by their feet, which he held with the greatest ease, one in each hand. Milo was so confounded with this second proof of his strength, that he turned up the whites of his eyes: O Jupiter, says he, thou hast sent us a second Hercules! Ælian. V. H. xii. 22. Titormus was also not a little famous as a trencherman.

[x] Conon, the Athenian general, we are to understand, was a very little man in person.

[y] The famous wrestler of Croton.

[z] A diminutive mortal mentioned by Aristophanes. Ornith. 1406.

could

could ever think of making [*a*] Perdiccas an Olympick champion, fit to contend with Theagenes the Thasian, or Polydamas, the [*b*] Scotussæan. They could do no more than undertake, where nature had not been wanting, to direct her efforts by the superaddition of art; of an art, the discovery of which were I to claim, I should not presume to make any such invidious promise, as that of taking the first man that offers, and metamorphosing him into an historian: at most I undertake to say, that, if a man has a natural turn for eloquence, and will take pains to improve his faculties, I can put him into a way more easily and more expeditiously to attain that which he aims at. You will not assert, that, where there is genius, there is no need of instruction; since you might as well say, that a man may become a very good harper, or piper, with-

[*a*] It is useless to inform the English reader, that two or three lines here in the original are not translated, being evidently an interpolation from the marginal note of some transcriber, wishing to satisfy himself who this Perdiccas could be.

[*b*] Scotussa was a town of Macedonia, on the river Nessus; but as to the champions, or their instructors, this annotator has nothing to say.

out

out ever learning to play on either inſtrument; or that, in ſhort, not to mince the matter, an univerſal ſcholar may become ſuch without any ſtudy or education whatever. Experience, however, ſufficiently ſhews, that nothing of the kind can be effected without a regular introduction and proper training. But only ſupply genius with tools for exerciſe, and practice ſoon makes perfect. Give me ſuch a diſciple as is not only quick to diſcern, but apt to expreſs his ideas; whoſe penetration is ſuch as would enable him to manage and direct real buſineſs, were he appointed to it; who has a turn for military as well as civil affairs, a mind informed by general experience and obſervation; in ſhort, one who has actually lived in a camp, and been converſant with every poſſible ſituation and diſcipline of an army. Let him be well acquainted with the ſeveral pieces of armour, and variety of machines made uſe of in war, and thoroughly inſtructed in the meaning of technical terms. He muſt underſtand the advantages to be reſpectively derived from every ſeparate form, order, movement, and manœuvre of an army. Upon the whole, he ſhould be ſuch an one as is fit for ſomething elſe beſides

fitting by a fire-fide, and liftening with open
mouth to other men's lies. Above all other
things, I would have him to be a man of the
moft liberal fentiments, who has nothing to
hope or to fear from any one. Otherwife our
hiftorian would not be a whit better than the
mercenary judge, who acquits or condemns juft
as he happens to be paid. He is not to be affected with the lofs of Philip's eye at the fiege of
Olynthus [c], by the arrow of After; but to

[c] The lofs of Philip's eye is mentioned by hiftorians as
having happened at the fiege of Methone, where a citizen of
Amphipolis, named After, offered him his fervices, declaring
himfelf fo expert an archer, that he could hit the fmalleft bird
flying. Philip thanked him very kindly, and told him he
fhould be glad of fuch an auxiliary, when he had a war with
the fwallows. The man was fo offended with this anfwer, that
he threw himfelf into the place, and immediately let fly an
arrow, with this infcription, " For Philip's right eye," which
eye was accordingly pierced by it. Philip returned the arrow, with another infcription, " If Philip take the town, he
will hang up After;" and having taken the town, he was as
good as his word. After this untoward accident, whoever
unfortunately mentioned a Cyclops in the prefence of Philip
was fure of giving that prince the greateft offence.

Pliny informs us, that, to conceal a like defect in the face
of king Antigonus, Apelles drew him in profile. If Philip's
painter was not equally polite, it was becaufe he did not
know his own intereft. Plin. XXXV. 10.

describe

describe him with all his imperfections on his head. He is not to be interested in the feelings of Alexander, who so cruelly murdered Clitus at an entertainment, but clearly to make known his character. Let not the noisy Cleon, who domineers on the bench, deter him, from affirming, that the [*d*] youth of Pella was a mischievous madman. Nor should the whole state of Athens biass him in relating their losses sustained in Sicily, the [*e*] captivity of Demosthenes, and the [*e*] death of Nicias; how they suffered from extreme thirst, what kind of water they were obliged to use, and what numbers were slain whilst they were drinking it. He will form this conclusion, than which nothing can be more just, that no man of sense will ever blame an author for describing things exactly as they were, though perhaps not so fortunate, nor so well conducted as might have been wished. For the historian is not to be considered as the cause, but as the relater of

[*d*] Unus Pellæo Juveni non sufficit orbis. Juvenal.

[*e*] Thucydides affirms, that both were slain in Sicily. Justin says, that Demosthenes fell by his own hand, and that Nicias suffered himself to be taken prisoner.

events. If his countrymen are beaten at sea, it is not he who sinks their ships; and, when they fly, he is not the man to [*f*] pursue. He has omitted no part of his duty, except perhaps a salutary vow. If concealment, or a different way of telling the story, could answer any purpose, it must have been a very easy matter for [*g*] Thucydides, with one stroke of his pen, to demolish the fortifications of Epipolæ, to sink the galley of Hermocrates, and to run that horrid Gylippus through the body, while he was employed in strengthening the works, and breaking up the roads. He might have driven the Syracusans to the quarries, and sent the Athenians on a voyage round Sicily and Italy, to fulfil the hopes of Alcibiades. But the misfortune is, that the fates themselves, I am afraid, would find it very hard to undo what is already done. The sole business of an historian is to recite occurrences in their natural order, just as they arose. But this he can never be expected to do, if he is afraid of

[*f*] Demosth. Olynth. III. 6.
[*g*] Thucyd. VI. and VII.

losing

losing his place as [b] Physician to Artaxerxes, or while he entertains hopes of wearing a [i] purple gown, or [i] a golden chain, or thinks of mounting a [i] Nisæan horse, as the reward of his praises. Far different is the conduct of Xenophon and Thucydides! Though both the one and the other had abundant cause to be angry, they nevertheless considered truth and the cause of the publick as too respectable to give place to [k] private animosity. Nor do they spare delinquents, though found amongst their friends. Whoever undertakes the province of an historian, as I have already observed, has nothing more to do than constantly to sacrifice to truth, regardless of the consequences. His only rule will be totally to neglect the opinions of the present age, and look forward to posterity. He who consults only the time present can be regarded in no other light than that of a sycophant, an office dis-

[b] See Plutarch's life of Artaxerxes.

[i] The Persians were not allowed the use of such fine things unless by special favour of the Prince. Xenoph. Cyrop. VIII.

[k] Both Xenophon and Thucydides were exiled by the influence of faction.

dained

dained by genuine history, from which flattery is as far distant as the arts of lasciviousness from the exercises of the palæstra. Very memorable is the saying of Alexander: "I wish, [*o*] Onesicritus," says he, "I could but revive for a little while after I am dead, if it were only to know how the publick will then be disposed to receive what you have written of me. While I am alive, it is no wonder that I should be so extravagantly praised. For praise is the great bait, with which every one hopes to make sure of me." Although Homer, in his frequent mention of Achilles, may seem often inclined to the fabulous, yet people are notwithstanding induced to believe what he says, because he wrote it after Achilles was dead; as they think there may be some reason for speaking the truth, when there can be no interest in telling a lie. Let our historian, I say, be without fear, unbiassed, perfectly free, open, and ingenuous, ready to communicate whatever he knows to be true, and calling, as it becomes him, a spade a spade. He is not to be the tributary of love, or hatred; not too merciful, too modest,

[*i*] A lying historian, who wrote the most incredible things in praise of Alexander.

or too shamefaced, to be hindered from giving
any man his due. He is to be an upright
judge, so far well-inclined to all the world,
as never to bestow on any one person in
it more than enough. In all his writings he is
to act the part of an impartial stranger, a citizen of the world, acknowledging no jurisdiction
superior to his own judgment, never once considering what his readers may say of him, but
only concerned to relate to them the real fact.
This was the rule which Thucydides prescribed
to himself, fairly to distinguish between the
right and the wrong, at a time when Herodotus was held in such great admiration, that
his several books were called by the names of
the nine Muses. " The thing is," says he,
rather to provide a lasting treasure, than to
catch at a momentary applause; to divest yourself of fable, and to transmit to after-ages an
exact transcript of what has truly come to
pass." He adds, that it is the general good,
which every sensible writer will propose to himself as the main end of history; " that, whenever similar circumstances may happen again
to arise, the reader may learn to make a right
use of them, by looking back to what he will
find

find already recorded." Let such be the disposition of my historian. As to language and the force of expression, he needs not aim at excessive vehemence, nor display such thundering periods, as if he meant to lay violent hands on his reader. Rather let that terrible sharpness of oratory yield to something more benign. Let his sentiments be concise and of a piece, his diction perspicuous and in general use, such as is best adapted to the elucidation of his subject. As we have proposed freedom of speech and ingenuous truth to direct our author's conduct, so let the first and great aim of his language be most clearly to explain and illustrate his matter, always rejecting the use of terms obscure or far remote from common life, and equally above copying the jargon of the mob. He must study to become master of such a mode of expression, as the learned shall approve, and the unlearned understand. Let there be no preposterous ornaments, no turgid and far-fetched allusions, which have the same effect on an author's style that too much seasoning has on soup. The historian's mind is to go along with his subject; and, when he is engaged in drawing up armies, and fighting

battles

battles by land or sea, he may fairly call in the aid of the poetical art, the better to exalt and elevate his story. On such occasions he will have need of the poetical afflatus, the better to fill his sails, and waft his towering bark over the summit of the waves. He may however in general vouchsafe to tread the earth, nor leave it, unless when raised aloft by the beauty and grandeur of his subject, to which he is evermore as much as possible to attach himself, but without once deviating into wildness, or suffering his imagination to be improperly heated. Which, whenever it happens, there is then the greatest danger of flying off and being furiously hurried away into downright poetry. The reins of the fancy are then to be held fast, and sobriety of sentiment carefully consulted; since too fiery a spirit is not more dangerous in the steed you cross than in the style you write. If you mount your Pegasus, it will be advisable to go a foot-pace, and hold fast, for fear of a fall. In the management of your words a due moderation is always to be regarded. Terms too distant, uncouth, and rough, are carefully to be avoided. Nor should your periods approach, as those of many historians
do,

do, to a perfect Rhythmus. The one is as much the effect of a false taste, as the other is unpleasant to the ear. The materials are not to be huddled together at random; great pains, and the most laborious diligence, being requisite in making a judicious selection. And you may very reasonably be allowed to rely most on what you have seen yourself. But where the testimony of your own eyes is not to be had, you are judiciously to collect the evidence of those who appear to be the least partial, the least likely to add to or diminish from the fact, from favour or dislike. A writer for this purpose must have a sufficient quickness of discernment, and be of abilities to make choice of what is most probable. When he has thus carefully collected all or the greatest part of his materials, let him draw out a sketch of the whole work, which, though yet imperfectly connected and unadorned, will be found a very useful note-book to begin with. To this, order and beauty and colouring are afterwards to be given; nor is any advantage to be omitted, which may result from an intimate acquaintance with the subject, from bestowing on it the dress that is most becoming, and making

all

all the parts in harmony with each other. Our impartial historian is to resemble Homer's Jupiter, who looks down one while upon [*m*] Thrace famous for horseflesh, and then casts an eye on [*n*] close-fighting Mysia. He is to take a distant survey of the Romans, just as they would appear to a spectator in the air above, and to relate their actions accordingly. Next he may turn his eyes to the Persians; or, if they are engaged in battle, on both at once. While the disposition is making for the fight, he is not to confine his attention to this or that particular, to this horseman, or that footman; unless indeed some [*o*] Brasidas should leap forward, or a [*o*] Demosthenes defend the pass. His first and principal regard must be had to the general officers: whatever orders they give he must know, and in what manner, and with what design, and for what end each disposition is made. When the two armies engage, he is to be an impartial spectator, weigh-

[*m*] Hom. Il. XIII. 4.

[*n*] Our author has omitted this epithet from Homer, which seems to be forgetting his own instructions, to give every one his due.

[*o*] Thucydides. IV.

ing

ing every thing on each fide in equal fcales, purfuing with the purfuers, and flying with thofe that fly. Let him never on any occafion forget when he is to leave off; nor, like an unexperienced boy, furfeit us with adventitious impertinence, but let him learn to acquit himfelf with propriety and eafe. Having firft duly fettled certain matters, he may then be free and difengaged, holding himfelf in readinefs to turn to that which may particularly demand his attention. And let him go on brifkly, in concord, as much as is poffible, with the occafion. He is to make nothing of a flight from Armenia into Media, from thence whizzing through the air into Iberia, and fo on to Italy, without lofs of time. The hiftorian's mind fhould refemble a mirrour, clean, clear, and [*p*] exact; that it may ex-

[*p*] ἀκριβῶς τὸ κάτοπτρον, exact in the centre. It is not very eafy to find out what is meant by this expreffion. Many conjectures have therefore been hazarded with refpect to the form, fafhion, and exiftence of fpeculums amongft the ancients. Of their exiftence there is as little doubt, as that the moderns have afcribed to their own invention many things which are not properly fo. Any polifhed body impervious to the rays of light is a mirror. A calm fea, if we may believe the poets, affords a very convenient toilet for an overgrown beau.

hibit

hibit things in their proper forms, and shew them such as they really are, without any perversion or variation either in colour or figure. His business is very different from that of the orator: he is in possession of his facts, and what he is instructed to say must be said at all events, and in due order. The question is how and not what he is to say. The composer of history is never to lose sight of its necessary resemblance to the performances of a Phidias, or Praxiteles, or Alcamenes. Those celebrated artists did not make the gold, or the silver, or the ivory, or any other materials they used; which were at all times ready prepared to their hands by the Elæans, or Athenians, or Argives. But their business was to fashion, to cut, to polish, to glue, to give the elegance and proportion. The historian's business is in like manner to make a finished display of his facts in the clearest and most becoming manner he is able. When the person who has heard such a work recited, is ready to believe he has himself seen the several events, and is therefore no niggard of his praise, then, and not till then, may our historical Phidias be assured, that his work is properly executed, and that the praise which he obtains is

no more than his lawful right. Having laid
in his stock of materials, he may sometimes
venture to begin without the formality of a
preface. For, if in any way the reader is made
acquainted with his design, he does in effect all
the business of a preface. However, when he
does write one, let it not be directed, like
those of the Rhetoricians, to [*q*] three considerations, since two will be found sufficient. If
he can make his reader attend, and beget in him
a disposition to be informed, he needs not give
himself any concern in bespeaking his favour.
For, who can forbear attending to him who
appears to deliver what is great, necessary, useful, and comes home to a man's own affairs?
And instruction will as certainly be conveyed by
a clearness of expression, by assigning the causes
of events, and properly marking out the chief
heads of his work. Such are the prefaces of
our best historians. With Herodotus the motive for writing is, " that the victories of the

[*q*] Attention, a disposition to be informed, and good will
to the speaker, were the three things aimed at by orators.

Greeks,

Greeks, and the defeats of the Barbarians, events in themselves great and wonderful, may not be forgotten and perish by time." Thucydides is of opinion, " that the war, which he relates, is of such consequence, as well deserves to be recorded; since it evidently exceeds all the former wars, and has been productive of the greatest calamities." The introduction should be longer or shorter, in proportion to the body of the work, to which we are to proceed by an easy and natural transition, and in which a long and continued narration is to be expected. Let it therefore proceed, dressed in its proper attire [r], fairly and softly, ever consistent with itself, admitting nothing extraneous, nor leaving out any thing to the purpose. In the language, let perspicuity evermore prevail, which depends, as I have already observed, on the connecting of one thing with another. This it is which will give the finishing to all; and, when the first intention is accomplished, will immediately introduce what comes next of course, in such a manner that the several circumstances and re-

[r] λειως και ὁμαλης τρεχετω.

lations will follow one another as uninterruptedly as the links of a chain, not like a bundle of stories preposterously put together at random, but all of a piece from the beginning to the end. Brevity and dispatch are always commendable, and especially when you have a superabundancy of matter. Nor do I mean so much to recommend a sparing of [*] words as of things; that is, when many trifling incidents occur of little or no consequence. By such prudent omissions, you will have the more room to enlarge on matters of great importance. Suppose you were to provide a sumptuous entertainment for your friends, consisting of every good dish and delicacy imaginable, of birds, and boars, and hares, and udders, and every thing else that is good, you would hardly, I suppose, after being so amply provided, think of serving up a sorry sprat, or a mess of water-gruel. In the midst of such plenty, I am confident, you would reject whatever is mean or indifferent. I could wish you

[*] No, Lucian, certainly not, if a body may judge by your own verbosity.

to be particularly on your guard against luxuriancy in your descriptions of mountains, walls, and rivers; nor suffer yourself to be tempted with a vain desire of shewing us what fine things you can say, neglecting your history to set off yourself. When you have said just as much as use and perspicuity require, and not a syllable more, learn then to pass on, avoiding the liquorish snares of flourish and affectation. Observe how Homer conducts himself in this respect. All poet as he is, how slightly nevertheless does he pass over Tantalus, Ixion, Tityus, &c. whereas, had the mention of Tantalus fallen in the way of Parthenius, or Euphorion, or [*] Callimachus, how many lines do you think it would have cost to get the water up to his lips? and how many verses do you suppose he would have employed in whirling Ixion's wheel? Observe how sparing Thucydides is in the use of this style, and how well he knows when to leave off, after describing a warlike machine, or a siege, the form of Epi-

[*] Callimachus, some of whose works are now extant, had such an aversion to long and tedious works, that to him is attributed that old and true saying, *a great book is a great evil.* He could not therefore be the Callimachus here censured.

polæ, or the port of Syracuse; not adding one
unneceffary word. If you think him tedious
in recounting the ravages of the peftilence, do
but attend to the variety and multiplicity of his
matter, and you will acknowledge, that the flying pen of the hiftorian is impeded by the numerous incidents crowding upon him. If you
fhould have occafion to introduce a profeffed
fpeech-maker, you will then have a fit opportunity of playing the rhetorician, and fhewing
the full power of your eloquence; but at the
fame time care muft be taken, that your orator
appear ftrictly in character, fpeak with propriety
and to the purpofe. Let your manner of diftri-
buting praife and blame be always moderate,
guarded, impartial and manly, accompanied
with fuitable proofs, diftributed briefly and fea-
fonably. Otherwife no attention will be paid to
what you fay, and you will be in the fame pre-
dicament with [a] Theopompus, who has fuch
a violent inclination to find fault, that he had
rather fuffer his hiftory to ftand ftill, than lofe
any opportunity of indulging his fpleen. If a

[a] Theopompus et Timæus duo maledicentiffimi. Cornelius Nepos, in Alcibiade. To fay every thing of
every body with the utmoft freedom, was the manner of
Theopompus. Cicero ad Attic. ii. 6.

wandering

wandering story chance to cross your way, you are to mention it not as a matter which you take upon you to be answerable for; but leave it to the reader to be determined, as he thinks best. Thus, by not leaning to either side, you are sure of being safe. Above all things remember the advice which I have so repeatedly given, not to confine your views to the praises and honours of the present age, but to take a far nobler and wider scope. Rejecting every temporary consideration boldly challenge futurity, write to ages unborn, and from them expect thy meed. Then shall it be said of thee: " This was a man unreserved, open, and ingenuous, who neither feared nor flattered any one, studious only of telling the plain truth." Ought not such a character as this in times to come far to outweigh all the little hopes of this short life? You have heard what is told of the architect of [x] Cnidus. After he had constructed the tower of [y] Pharos, that most beautiful and capital work, that mariners at a distance, seeing the lighthouse,

[x] A city of Caria, in Asia minor.
[y] A small island at the mouth of the Nile, in which was a tower with lights to direct vessels in the night.

might

might at the fame time be fenfible of their own
danger, and avoid the fatal rocks of [z] Paræ-
tonia;—having finifhed this amazing work, he
cut his name in the folid ftone, over which he
then put a coat of plafter, and infcribed on the
furface the name of the then reigning king; well
knowing (as it actually came to pafs) that in a little time the letters would moulder away with the
furface on which they were written, leaving for all
men to read on the lafting rock, "Softratus the
"Cnidian, fon of Dexiphanes, to the Gods pre-
"ferving voyagers by fea." You fee he paid
no manner of regard to the time then prefent,
nor once thought of the fhort period of his own
life; but ventured to look forwards to our
days, and to every future age, as long as the
monument of his art fhould remain. In like
manner whoever undertakes the province of
hiftory is fteadily to adhere to the truth, which,
though it afford but a future and diftant hope,
is much preferable to the fond flattery, which he
might think immediately to obtain by a contrary
conduct. Let this therefore be thy rule, this

[z] Paræonia, or Patætonium, a large a city of Ægypt.

the

the only guide, on which thou mayeſt depend. Whoever cloſes with theſe directions cannot fail to compaſs his end. And whoever neglects them will unavoidably fall into the errors which he has been cautioned to avoid, and I ſhall have laboured to as little purpoſe as Diogenes rolling his tub.

To gratify any remaining curiosity of the Reader, who by this time has had enough of translation, the following enumeration of all the Dialogues and other works of Lucian is here subjoined, in the same order in which they are printed in the Amsterdam Edition of 1743.

1. THE Dream; or, the Life of Lucian. Vol. I. p. 1. 2d ed.

2. The Author's apology for his manner of writing to one who had called him Prometheus. Prometheus was a dealer in dirt.

3. Nigrinus. Exposes the vicious lives of philosophers and others.

4. The Judgment of the vowels. Sigma, a Greek consonant, brings an action against his neighbour Tau before the bench of vowels, complaining of the violence and injustice of him the said Tau.

5. Timon: or, the Man-hater. Vol. I. p. 17. 2d ed.

6. The Kingfisher. Vol. II. p. 332.

7. Prometheus: or, Caucasus. Our author's several dialogues of the gods are in general an abstract of whatever is most entertaining in the fables concerning them, at the same time that they fail not to point out what was more particularly ridiculous. One of the remaining tragedies of Æschylus is on this story of Prometheus. Prometheus there complains, as he does here, though not in the same manner, how scandalously Jupiter has treated him. To nail him to a rock for a mere convivial jest, was very scurvy usage in any God who pretends to know what it is to keep good company! and to punish him for being his friend was still worse!

8. Prometheus and Jupiter. Vol. II. p. 205.
9. Cupid and Jupiter. Vol. II. p. 20.
10. Jupiter and Mercury.
11. Jupiter and Ganymede.
12. Juno and Jupiter.
13. Juno and Jupiter.
14. Apollo and Vulcan. Vol. II. p. 212.
15. Vulcan and Jupiter. Vol. II. p. 216.

16. Nep-

16. Neptune and Mercury. Vol. II. p. 219.
17. Mercury and the Sun.
18. Venus and the Moon.
19. Venus and Cupid.
20. Jupiter, Æsculapius and Hercules. Vol. II. p. 188.
21. Mercury and Apollo.
22. Apollo and Mercury.
23. Juno and Latona.
24. Apollo and Mercury.
25. Juno and Jupiter.
26. Venus and Cupid.
27. The Judgment of the Goddesses. Jupiter, Mercury, Juno, Minerva, Venus, Paris. The Judgment of Paris is a story well known.
28. Mars and Mercury. Vol. II. p. 185.
29. Pan and Mercury.
30. Apollo and Bacchus.
31. Mercury and Maia.
32. Jupiter and the Sun. Vol. II. p. 223.
33. Apollo and Mercury.
34. Doris and Galatea. This and the fourteen following are called Sea Dialogues.
35. Cyclops and Neptune. Vol. II. p. 202.
36. Alpheus and Neptune.

37. Me-

37. Menelaus and Proteus. Vol. II. p. 199.
38. Panope and Galene.
39. Triton, Amymone, Neptune.
40. Notus and Zephyrus.
41. Neptune and the Dolphins. Vol. II. p. 196.
42. Neptune and the Nereids. Vol. II. p. 194.
43. Iris and Neptune.
44. Xanthus and the Sea. Vol. II. p. 191.
45. Doris and Thetis.
46. Neptune and Enipeus.
47. Triton and the Nereids.
48. Zephyrus and Notus.
49. Diogenes and Pollux. Vol. II. p. 180.
50. Pluto; a complaint against Menippus. Vol. II. p. 177.
51. Menippus, Amphilochus, and Trophonius. Vol. II. p. 174.
52. Mercury and Charon. Vol. II. p. 171.
53. Pluto and Mercury. Vol. II. p. 168.
54. Terpsion and Pluto. Vol. II. p. 163.
55. Zenophantes and Callimedes. Vol. II. p. 160.
56. Knemon and Damnippus. Vol. II. p. 158.

57. Si-

57. Simylus and Polyftratus. Vol. II. p. 152.
58. Charon, Mercury, and feveral of the dead. Vol. II. p. 139.
59. Crates and Diogenes. Vol. II. p. 135.
60. Alexander, Annibal, Minos, and Scipio. Vol. II. p. 125.
61. Diogenes and Alexander. Vol. II. p. 120.
62. Alexander and Philip. Vol. II. p. 114.
63. Achilles and Antilochus. Vol. II. p. 111.
64. Diogenes and Hercules. Vol. II. p. 105.
65. Menippus and Tantalus. Vol. II. p. 102.
66. Menippus and Mercury.
67. Æacus, Protefilaus, Menelaus, and Paris.
68. Menippus, Æacus, Pythagoras, Empedocles, and Socrates. Vol. II. p. 93.
69. Menippus and Cerberus. Vol. II. p. 91.
70. Charon, Menippus, and Mercury. Vol. II. p. 82.
71. Pluto and Protefilaus. Vol. II. p. 87.
72. Diogenes and Maufolus. Vol. II. p. 79.
73. Nireus, Therfites, and Menippus. Vol. II. p. 77.

74. Me-

74. Menippus and Chiron. Vol. II. p. 73.

75. Diogenes, Antisthenes, and Crates. Vol. II. p. 65.

76. Menippus and Tiresias.

77. Ajax and Agamemnon. Vol. II. p. 62.

78. Minos and Sostratus. Vol. II. p. 57.

79. Menippus and Philonides. Menippus is just returned from a visit to the wits in the other world, and gives his friend an account of what he has seen there. Pride, he tells him, has had a fall, and the fortune of the rich and great is totally reversed. Of mighty sovereigns, he says, some beg their bread; others, who are at last inclined to be useful, cry salt-fish, or cobble shoes. Philip of Macedon, for instance, is squat in a corner, where he handles the awl—rather awkwardly, one may suppose. Such as can read turn schoolmasters, and teach little children their A B C. What is meant to be inculcated is, that the condition of private persons is the most eligible. Λαθι βιωσας. "Steal through the world."

80. Charon: or, the Observers. Vol. I. p. 71. 2d ed.

81. Of Sacrifices. Vol. II. p. 227.

82. The

82. The Sale of Lives. Vol. II. p. L

83. The fisherman. Lucian apologizes for what he had written againſt philoſophers, ſaying he never meant thoſe who were really ſuch. He compares the pretended teachers of wiſdom and virtue to certain Ægyptian apes, which were taught to dance, and performed with great gravity and applauſe, till they were unluckily ſeduced from their duty by a man of humour throwing a handful of nuts amongſt them.

84. The Infernal Paſſage. Vol. I. p. 113. 2d. ed.

85. On the wretched condition of thoſe who waſte their time and proſtitute their talents in a ſervile dependency on the great.

86. Lucian, having got a place at court, makes as good an excuſe as he can for his own inconſiſtency.

87. An apology for ſaying *vywne* at meeting a friend inſtead of χαῖρε. *Tyune* means farewel, which cuſtom has confined to parting.

88. Hermotimus: of the ſects of Philoſophers. Expoſes their jarring pretenſions and ſenſeleſs diſdain of one another.

89. He-

89. Herodotus: or, Action. An introductory speech before a recital of his works in Macedonia.

90. Zeuxis: or, Antiochus. An addrefs to the criticks.

91. Literary appeals are to be made to competent judges.

92. The Scythian Stranger. Toxaris introduced his countryman Anacharfis to Solon at Athens, with lefs advantage to him than Lucian is received in Macedonia.

93. Of the manner in which Hiftory ought to be written. Vol. II. p. 340.

94. The true Hiftory; in two parts. This true Hiftory is as true as the travels of our ingenious countryman Sir John Mandeville, and not greatly inferior in other refpects to the remains of that illuftrious knight.

95. The Tyrant-killer. A perfon flew the fon of a tyrant; which having occafioned the tyrant to lay violent hands on himfelf, the perfon claims the reward affigned by the law to a tyrant-killer.

96. The Difinherited Son. A difinherited fon ftudies phyfick, and cures his father of madnefs,

madness, after being given over by other phyficians. He is then received into favour; but, on his refusal to cure his stepmother of the same distemper, he is disinherited a second time. This is his defence.

97. Phalaris I. The Manifesto of Phalaris, on offering his brazen bull to the priests of Delphi.

98. Phalaris II. A priest advises his brethren not to be so uncharitable as to refuse his present.

99. Alexander: or, the false prophet. The history of an impostor.

100. Of Dancing. A defence of the art.

101. Lexiphanes. Ridicules the affected use of hard words.

102. The Eunuch. Whether such a person is fit for the study of philosophy.

103. Of Astrology. A Defence of the art.

104. Demonax. The life of a philosopher, Lucian's friend.

105. The Loves.

106. The Images. The idea of an accomplished woman.

107. A Defence of the Images.

108. Tox-

108. Toxaris. An enquiry whether Greece or Scythia has afforded greater examples of friendship.

109. Lucius; or, the Ass.

110. Jupiter confuted.

111. Jupiter in Tragedy. Ridicules the Gods for not punishing the impudence of Philosophy.

112. The Dream: or, the Cobler and his Cock. Vol. I. ed. 2. p. 157.

113. Icaromenippus. Vol. I. ed. 2. p. 209.

114. The Double Indictment. Sprightly Dialogue preferable to crabbed ignorance.

115. The Parasite. A panegyrick on the art of living at another man's expence.

116. Of Exercises. Vol. I. ed. 2. p. 247.

117. Of mourning for the dead. The folly of it.

118. The Master of Rhetoricians. Ironical satire.

119. The Incredulous. Ridicules the several tales about ghosts, charms, &c.

120. Hippias; or, the Bath. A description of one.

121. Bac-

121. Bacchus: a preface.

122. Hercules: a preface.

123. Of Amber: or, the Swans. The transformation of Phaeton's sisters into poplars distilling amber, no less than that of Apollo's companions into swans, a fiction of the poets.

124. An encomium on Flies. Oil is poison to them.

125. To an illiterate owner of a vast library.

126. That we ought not hastily to give credit to scandalous stories.

127. Pseudoligistes. A defence of the word Apophras, the black day, to which he likens his opponent.

128. A Description of a Fine House.

129. An account of several persons, who lived to a great age.

130. On the love of our native country.

131. Dipsas. A compliment.

132. On Poetical Inspiration. Vol. I. ed. 2. p. 293.

133. The Ship: or, the Wishes. Vol. II. p. 242.

134. Dialogues of the Courtezans. In these Dialogues, which are fifteen in number, the ladies converse together like themselves.

D d

135. Of the death of Peregrinus.

136. The Fugitives. Vol. II. p. 293.

137. The Saturnalia. The Carnival of Antiquity.

138. Chronosolon. The laws of the Saturnalia.

139. Saturnalian Epistles. These epistles are four in number. The first is from a poor man to Saturn, intreating him to use his interest with the rich, that the lower sort of people may be permitted to share in the good things of this world. Epistle the second is Saturn's reply. He assures the poor man of his readiness to serve him in any thing in his power, but begs him not to entertain so extravagant an opinion of the happiness of being rich. In the third epistle Saturn advises the rich to behave better to the poor, assuring them that they will find their account in so doing. The fourth epistle is the defence made by the rich. They would be very glad, they say, to admit the poor to their houses and familiarity, as formerly, provided they would learn better manners, and not abuse their good-nature.

140. The Feast: or, the Lapithæ. A quarrel at a wedding-dinner. The philosophers standing up, every one for his own sect, at last
fell

fell to blows, in order to determine which was the beft.

141. Of the Syrian Goddefs. A defcription of the temple and religious ceremonies of a city in Syria.

142. The praifes of Demofthenes.

143. The Council of the Gods. Vol. I. ed. 2. p. 303.

144. The Cynick. Vol. I. ed. 2. p. 321.

145. The Pfeudofophift: or, the Solœcift. Of the want of propriety in fpeaking Greek, and the ignorance of thofe who pretend to underftand it beft.

146. Philopatris: or, the Learner.

147. Charidemus. Of Beauty.

148. Nero: or, the cutting the Ifthmus. Nero's extravagancies.

149. The Gout: a Tragedy.

150. Ocypus. Ocypus was a flout young fellow, who ufed to laugh at perfons afflicted with the gout, but found at laft that mocking was catching.

151. Epigrams. Lucian is fuppofed to be repeating the firft of thofe epigrams in the frontifpiece. There is a tranflation of it at the beginning of the former Volume.

IT is to be observed, that many of the pieces here enumerated, and which are commonly printed with the works of Lucian, are by the best judges supposed not to be his.

Though I have not deemed it necessary to be blind to my author's imperfections, I cannot take leave of the indulgent Reader without whispering in his ear a secret, to go no further; that this translation conveys no adequate idea of the wit of Lucian.

J. C.

END OF THE SECOND VOLUME.

www.ingramcontent.com/pod-product-compliance
Lightning Source LLC
Chambersburg PA
CBHW030546300426
44111CB00009B/870